GOVERNING IN SCARY TIMES

The Board's Roadmap for Governing Through and Beyond an Emergency

DR. DEBRA L. BROWN,
DAVID A. H. BROWN
AND
ROB DEROOY

ISBN: 978-1-64746-672-5 (Paperback)
ISBN: 978-1-64746-673-2 (Hardback)
ISBN: 978-1-64746-674-9 (Ebook)

More Governance Resources to Help You Govern in Scary Times

Earn Your Professional Director® Designation

The Professional Director Education and Certification Program® is a world-class, **online director education program** where you can build competence and confidence in governance while you earn a Pro.Dir® designation. Whether you work for a small company or a Fortune 500 enterprise; are a board member, senior executive or provide support to a board; serve in the private, public or not-for-profit sector; have a little, some, or a lot of governance experience; this program will build the confidence, skills, knowledge and competence in governance you need to make it in today's complex boardroom. www.professionaldirector.com

Evaluate Your Board and CEO

The Board Evaluation Solution is a best practice, comprehensive, **online board evaluation suite** that is second to none! Leveraging our many years of board evaluation experience, this suite lets you easily and clearly identify areas for action and improvement. You can select evaluation of the board, its committees, the board and committee chairs, and individual director peer and self-evaluations — or any combination of these! All reports give you comprehensive results and benchmarked scorecards in key dimensions of board effectiveness. www.governancesolutions.ca

The CEO Evaluation Solution is an online CEO evaluation tool that makes this task as easy as 1, 2, 3! Get confidential, objective, professional results. Our tool evaluates the CEO in three distinct ways: against accountabilities; against the results and outcomes of goals, objectives and targets; and against their leadership qualities. www.governancesolutions.ca

Optimize Your Governance

Governance Consulting and Coaching will propel and optimize your governance effectiveness and lead to superior corporate results. You can expect clear outcomes, objective assessment, helpful advice and actionable strategies. Whether you need a comprehensive governance review, one-on-one coaching in governance skills, team coaching to enhance board solidarity, or help with that difficult director, our consultants can be trusted to be discreet, sensitive and practical. www.governancesolutions.ca

Organize with Your Board Portal

BoardConnex® is the latest in board portal solutions provided by the savvy technology team of Sandbox Software Solutions and the governance experts at Governance Solutions. This secure, web-based online board portal makes it easy and convenient for you to oversee your organization with confidence. Integrate governance resources, advice and collaboration tools with meeting and document management! www.boardconnex.com

Contact us today! contact@governancesolutions.ca

To all those impacted by COVID-19

With special thanks to our editor Lorna Stuber and those on the Governance Solutions Team who made this book possible: Vicki Dickson, Alex Martin, Rafael Mazotine, Dave McComiskey and Jake Skinner

CONTENTS

INTRODUCTION

In April 2020, about six weeks into the state of emergency caused by the COVID-19 pandemic, we asked 375 board members two questions:

1. To what extent has this pandemic and resulting state of emergency effected your organization?
2. How different do you expect the organization to look once the pandemic is well behind us?

The results were stunning! A full 89% reported they had already been affected to one extent or the other with 76% of those negatively so. And 93% said that they expected their organization to be forever changed, with almost 20% of those expecting the permanent changes to be significant. This means that at a minimum, 93% of boards will need to relook their plans and the governance of their organizations! And, we suspect, so too will the other 7%! This book is based on a series of governance education sessions provided at the height of the 2020 pandemic to board chairs, board members, CEOs, C-Suite Executives and staff that support the governance functions of organizations across private, public and not-for-profit sectors.

In this publication we review the content of those sessions, which covered these topics:

- Strategic Planning in the New Economy

- Unwinding from the Crisis — The Risks and the Opportunities

- Attracting and Retaining the Best Employees in the New Economy

- Catching Up with the New Reality — Reshaping Policies and Protocols

- Refreshing the Financials and Projecting What Comes Next

- Taking Stock — Monitoring the Financial Impacts

- Compliance — How Well Did We Do and What Would We Do Differently in the Future?

- Evaluating How We Did — Board and CEO Evaluations Post-Crisis

- The New Corporate Performance Scorecard — Setting a New Standard

- Reinforcing Confidence with Your Stakeholders — Keep the Conversation Going

Each of the sessions included a list of questions that board members should be considering as they govern and navigate through and beyond COVID-19. Those too are included in this book for your use!

This ten-part series is framed in the context of board governance and the role of the board. It has been designed not as ten random topics of interest but as ten systematic governance steps that boards will need to take on their journey through and beyond the current crisis. For each of these steps we provide a series of important questions that you are going to want to ask and answer.

To begin, we start with the fundamental definition of governance that comes from the Cadbury Report and the UK Corporate Governance Code, which is "governance is the system by which organizations are directed controlled."[1] Beyond this definition, probably the most important line in the 1992 Cadbury Report that still rings true today around the world in all sectors, is that the "board of directors is responsible for the governance of the firm."[2]

The system, which we have developed and articulated through almost 30 years of research, outlines the five levels of direction and of control that the board is responsible for. The board of directors has the responsibility to set direction and then to gain confidence that the organization is going in that direction, which is what is meant by control.

---

[1]   Sir Adrian Cadbury, *The Financial Aspects of Corporate Governance*, Report of the Committee on the Financial Aspects of Corporate Governance with Code of Best Practice (London: Gee Publishing, 1992), 14.

[2]   Cadbury, *The Financial Aspects of Corporate Governance*, 14.

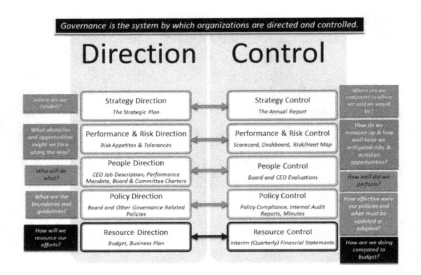

The highest level of setting direction is strategy, and that involves setting and approving the long-term, strategic direction of the organization. Where are you headed?

The second layer or level of direction is performance and risk. What are the obstacles and opportunities that you might face along the way, and how do you plan to mitigate and or capitalize on those? That is called performance and risk direction, which the board approves.

The third layer of governance is people direction. The most important question in people direction has to do with the CEO. This is about who will do what in the organization, making sure that you put in place the board's one employee, the chief executive officer or executive director, who is going to be responsible to run the organization day-to-day between board meetings and within their delegated authority.

That brings us to layer four: policy direction. This doesn't just happen in a vacuum. The board approves a small number of high-level policies that define the boundaries and guidelines of how management is to act and operate the organization between board meetings versus what they need to bring back to the board for approval.

And then finally, resource direction is the fifth level, which is largely articulated through the budget because the budget is how you pay for everything. That is, how do you resource the efforts in the directional plan? The budget is the way in which you pay for human resources, tangible resources as well as other resources.

Those are the five layers of direction. And there are parallel levels of control or gaining reasonable assurance or confidence that you are headed in that direction.

What we plan to do in this book is to walk you through these ten steps or ten roles that the board has. We start with the highest level of direction: the board's role in strategic planning in the new economy. Then, we look at unwinding from the crisis: the risks and opportunities. What's the board's role in that? Next, we look at attracting and retaining the best employees in the new economy: the people direction. There are significant shifts there for us to consider. This is followed with a look at how the new reality is reshaping policies and protocols and the impacts on refreshing the financial projections of the organization to ensure a clear budget and resource allocations going forward.

Those chapters cover the directional side of governance — the board's governance roles in setting direction. The second half of the book covers the board's role in gaining confidence or reasonable assurance, starting with taking a stock of and monitoring the financial impacts. What are some of the key financial ratios that you should be looking at going forward? Then we move on to compliance. How well did you do, particularly in business continuity and crisis communication planning? Are there some policies that you need to rewrite or update? What would, or should you do differently? Next, we ask if it's time to evaluate: how do you deal with board and CEO evaluations post-crisis coming through and beyond? Assessing results and the new corporate performance scorecard comes next. Lastly, we discuss how to reinforce confidence with your stakeholders.

This ties together all the different governance threads boards should be concerned with as they govern beyond COVID.

CHAPTER 1
STRATEGIC PLANNING IN THE NEW ECONOMY

As leaders, your thoughts have likely been focused primarily on four immediate pressures of late:

- the health and safety of your employees
- ensuring business continuity
- risks to your reputation, and
- stakeholder communications.

You will have moved on beyond the immediacy of these to assessing the impacts and ensuring board and management discussions, and decisions have been properly implemented and documented. You have been doing things on the fly, and you want to make sure that you have crossed your T's and dotted your I's. You are keeping an eye on reopening plans and activities, and you are thinking and planning for beyond the emergency. Some of you may even be fully operational or have grown exponentially through the pandemic. The crisis has had many negative effects. But we are glass-half-full kind of people! We make lemonade out of lemons and know we will find good in most circumstances if we just look for it.

In this chapter, we will examine the following themes:

Theme 1: Urgent Pressure to Concurrently Think Concurrently Through Multiple Timelines

Theme 2: A Singular Unique Opportunity to Lead in the Shaping of Culture

Theme 3: Cognitive Biases — Especially Pessimism, Optimism and Discounting Biases

Theme 4: Multiple Industry Shakeups

Theme 5: Compelling Need for Vision Casting to Give People Hope

Theme 6: Demand for Adaptability and Resiliency in the Organization

Theme 7: Excellence in Crisis Communications

Theme 8: Collaboration and Opportunity with Competition

Theme 9: Significant Rapid Innovation

Theme 1: Urgent Pressure to Think Concurrently Through Multiple Timelines

One positive result of the crisis is that it has caused virtually every board to systematically think and reflect on the impacts of the pandemic. This has led them to turn their attention to the longer term and to enhanced governance. Your CEO and board have shifted, rethought strategic priorities and recalibrated and retooled for the new economy, the new marketplace. The crisis has caused leaders to think concurrently about multiple timelines.

If your organization isn't thinking about all four of the following levels concurrently, you need to.

This is the first question for your toolkit:

How well is our organization currently thinking about all four of these timelines?

o *reacting to the crisis (to survive)*

o *recalibrating in the aftershock (to stabilize)*

o *rebounding to the new realities (to sustain)*

o *reimagining the future (to succeed)*

It is hard enough in normal times for us to think about one timeline, the timeline that we're in. Now we are having to think in four streams all at the same time.

Theme 2: A Singular Unique Opportunity to Lead in the Shaping of Culture

The second theme that we are seeing is that this is a singular unique opportunity to shape culture. Culture is formed, embedded, shaped and changed through shared experience.

Full stop. Shared experience is how you change culture. If you are not leading your culture, your culture is leading you. There is no better time to lead in shaping your culture than now. This is why: everybody in your organization is sharing the experience of maneuvering through this pandemic, not just you and your employees. Your entire board, leadership team, customers and suppliers are part of this shared experience. Everyone who is attached to your organization is going through the same shared experience — simultaneously.

We are living in the days where the best approach is, like Nike says, "Just do it." Leaders are jump-starting to "yes!" Governments have been able to make quick decisions and implement complex solutions to deliver major programs in record time. Big moves that have been stalled or in the works for years are suddenly becoming quick "yeses." Moves like shutting down a large office or closing branches happen at the stroke of a pen. For example, our local branch bank has temporarily closed. We doubt it will ever reopen.

Bureaucracy, low risk tolerance, lack of innovation or other cultural issues have prevented companies from moving quickly with the speed and agility needed to transform. Suddenly, their response has become, "Just do it." In some cases, it has been, "Let's just try anything!" Pre-COVID inefficiencies have created post-COVID survival movements. Here's the thing: you can only change culture as quickly as your culture will allow.

The shared experience of this crisis has provided a unique opportunity for real culture change.

The shared experience of this crisis has provided a unique opportunity for real culture change. Everyone at the same time is recognizing the need for such change. A controversial example is with schoolteachers. Where we live, just prior to the pandemic, teachers were fighting online learning for all they were worth. They wanted no part of it. The pandemic forced them into it. Now, many are embracing it. Many are finding value in it. And, dare we day, some are enjoying it!

Not every organization is looking for culture change. You may have a very healthy culture. However, if you are looking for culture change, there is no better time than now. Culture change typically needs two ingredients: shared experience and a burning platform. So often when we try to change our culture, we must fabricate a perceived burning platform to convince people of the need for change. Too, we find ourselves dragging people along, at times kicking and screaming. With the pandemic, we have an immediate burning platform. Most people are ready to jump together. We are faced with one big, collective, shared experience and burning platform. If there was ever a time to lead through the reshaping of your culture, that time is now.

Why are we talking about culture in a chapter devoted to strategy? You have likely heard this expression, often attributed to management thinker, Peter Drucker: "Culture eats strategy for breakfast." In other words, unless and until your culture is aligned and healthy, you are not going to be able to effectively and efficiently achieve strategy.

Two more questions in your toolkit are as follows:

How aligned, healthy and effective is our organizational culture going forward?

How might we use this opportunity to lead in culture formation?

Seventy-five percent of people in our poll said that they expect their organization to be different to some extent after we are through this crisis. Eighteen percent expect their organization to be significantly different. That means 93%

of those organizations can expect their culture to change. The question becomes, "What will it change to?"

Leaders must guide, enable and facilitate those changes to line up with values and strategy. The CEO is the head of culture. They are the one who stamps, champions, leads and changes the culture. It is the responsibility of the board to oversee organizational culture by ensuring the CEO is moving the organization in the right direction.

When going through a crisis, organizations operate in "war time" governance. In "war time" governance, everybody unites against the common enemy. People are more willing to let leaders lead when they are at war. Your opportunity to change culture is now, not after the war is over. You need to act quickly. There is a burning platform. The board and CEO need to persevere and use this opportunity to craft culture, or it will just slip back when the crisis is behind us. It will quickly revert.

Theme 3: Cognitive Biases — Especially Pessimism, Optimism and Discounting Biases

Part of the reason for reverting back to previous habits, and related to this discussion about culture, is cognitive and unconscious biases. There is significant research on literally dozens of cognitive biases. They are not all bad! We develop unconscious biases to solve our problems. The need for problem solving is why cultures develop in the first place. Cognitive biases, like a lot of aspects of culture, are unconscious. Our job is to shine light on them to understand them. When we understand them, we can figure out which ones are at play and ask ourselves, "Do we need to challenge this bias?" Some biases are unhealthy and contribute to an unhealthy culture in the boardroom as well as the organization.

There are three cognitive biases that have been heightened during this crisis. One is a pessimism bias. This is when a board member is likely to exaggerate the negative effects of long-term outcomes. These board members will be reluctant to make any changes and will lean towards reverting to the old culture, believing it will be safer, more predictable. They may think, "Let's just see if we can ride this thing out."

The opposite bias is an optimism bias. Those with an optimism bias are more likely to argue that the current problems will pass and the future will hold more promise. Therefore, we should adapt and change our culture to lean into that promise of the future. In the context of this emergency, those with an optimism bias are more likely to be the ones protesting in the street to open the restaurants, open the beaches, stop the lockdown and allow everyone to get back to work! At the same time, people with pessimism bias protest, "No, no changes, no changes to the lockdown. Do not even open up a little bit; stay where we are." They are concerned about things getting worse and worse.

There is a third cognitive bias we are seeing in boardrooms today, and that is called discounting. What we mean by discounting is that people are more responsive to immediate consequences than delayed ones, but at the same time, board members may hesitate to implement tough decisions because the adverse consequences are immediate.

Boards with this bias must be careful not to hesitate. This is the opportunity to leverage this bias, to embrace culture change where you need to. Embrace it where it's going to be a healthy and needful change because employees and the rest of your stakeholders will more readily accept culture change now. There is a heightened awareness. We are in war governance. We have a burning platform. This is the time to be more open at a board level to the leadership of the CEO in major transformation and culture change efforts.

How do you handle these biases in the boardroom? Be aware of them and make decisions based on facts, not feelings.

Here are two more question to put in your toolkit:

How well have we recognized and challenged any potential cognitive biases that could negatively impact our strategy?

How confident are we that our decisions are based on facts rather than a pessimism, optimism or discounting bias?

Theme 4: Multiple Industry Shakeups

Another theme affecting boardrooms today is shakeup in many industries. For example, we see a shakeup in the digital landscape. COVID-19 has accelerated this shift. Transitional shifts are taking only days, weeks or months when previously they may have taken months or years. Some organizations like Zoom and other online meeting software companies, eCommerce companies, cybersecurity companies and internet providers are getting immediate benefits. They are on the upside of this crisis. Yet, in that same industry there are companies that are facing significant challenges. For example, IT infrastructure companies are on the other side of this. They have negative pressure on their supply chains and the work from home movement.

It is not just the digital space experiencing shakeup. Travel, tourism, financial services, healthcare, education and dozens more are also impacted. The work at home movement is affecting almost every industry. We know executives in large companies who have been working from home for months now. Many say they are never going back to the office again. Some say their teams have never been as connected and accountable as they are now. They are more productive, less depleted from long commutes, and happier in general. How is that going to shake up industry, and how is it going to impact the boardroom? How will the board assess and make decisions during these types of shakeups?

There are tools typically used in strategic thinking that will help. First, we should differentiate between strategic thinking and strategic planning. Many organizations jump straight into strategic planning. This is the conversation about forecasting and evaluating agreements on priorities going forward. Strategic thinking is what we do before we plan. Strategic thinking is divergent thinking — ideation to come up with alternatives.

Which products and services are being delivered by which channel (e.g. in person, online) into which markets? How has this changed? How will it change?

There are a couple of tools that you can use here. One is called I-scan (internal scan). Internal scans look at your organization and ask what has changed regarding human resources, financial resources and technical, including technological, resources. They ask, "What do we expect to change coming through this?" So, for example, the issue of working from home is one piece to look at. What does that social covenant with your employees look like? And what about online delivery of products and services? Many sectors have shifted from in-person to online delivery. Somebody skilled in I-scanning should be assembling a good evaluation of internal resources and how those resources have shifted.

A second tool related to strategic thinking is called product-market matrix. This is a tool used to analyze and plan growth strategies. A simple table is designed in a way that allows an organization to generate four alternate strategic directions.

Product-Market Matrix Example

Market \\ Product	Canada Retail	Canada Wholesale	USA Retail	USA Wholesale	Online
T-shirts	✓	✓			✓ NEW
Sweaters	✓				✓ NEW
Shoes	✓		✓	✓	✓ NEW

The tools are implemented by management. The role of the board in the implementation is to receive reporting from management on the application on the tools. The board uses the findings to make more informed decisions. With these tools, you can have a good dialogue about strategic thinking before you even get to the convergence of strategic planning.

Theme 5: Compelling Need for Vision Casting to Give People Hope

Another theme we are seeing is the increased need to cast vision. People need and are looking for hope during a short-term focus on the immediate crisis. One of my favourite books says that "where there is no vision, the people perish."[3] While we are all laser focused on the tactical, our employees need to catch a glimpse of where they are going. They need leaders who will raise their sights and give them something across the horizon to focus on. They need to see beyond the day-to-day. The team needs to see that there is a plan and that there is a real target beyond the immediate crisis.

That target is your long-term vision. Encourage people to reaffirm and refocus on that vision. Especially during a crisis, people need courage. The word encourage literally

---

[3]   Proverbs 29:18 (King James Version).

means to "give courage." Encourage your team members with vision.

This is not about reinventing the wheel. In our book *Governance Solutions*, Chapter 5 explains the board's role in strategic thinking and planning. It covers what we call the horizon plan. This includes the vision, mission and values. This is the horizon, the frame within which we are going to conduct strategic planning, business planning and operational planning. We are not talking about starting over. Rather, the horizon plan involves looking at your vision, mission and values and answering the following questions:

To what extent do the vision, mission and values continue to reflect the organization in terms of its horizon point?

What is possible?

How might we adopt shaping and visionary strategies to influence and exploit the post-crisis landscape?

If the answer is, they do not adequately line up with where you are headed as an organization, the organization will need to embark on a journey to rearticulate a vision, mission and values.

Theme 6: Demand for Adaptability and Resiliency in the Organization

Another theme that we are seeing is the need for adaptability and resiliency. A great example is the forecasting and modeling that we have seen related to COVID. We only see the tip of the iceberg on the news. Every government and organization is trying to get a handle on what is a moving target. The point is, we need accurate predictions in the boardroom to make good decisions. At the same time, we need to understand that we can't be married to those predictions. There is a lot of uncertainty in a crisis.

Recently we spoke with Barry Rempel, the CEO of Winnipeg Airport Authority. He recounted that when COVID first hit, they predicted they would experience as much as a 50% reduction in activity at the airport. Two months later he said, "Oh, that we only had a 50% reduction!" There is this moving target boards are attempting to hit. While you are restarting, reinventing, downsizing and upsizing, you need projections; but in the boardroom, in a crisis, you can't be married to them. You must be able to adapt.

To the extent that your organization faces a host of uncertainties, it is easy to throw your hands in the air and say, "I don't really know how we're going to forecast or project." The tool that you want to use for this is called scenario planning.

Scenario planning should be led by a skilled person on staff — someone who is a good storyteller, who can grasp and assemble complex variables and turn them into a short, punchy, interesting story or narrative. Each of the scenarios is archetypal. In other words, they are not just variances of one another. They are significantly different from one another asking questions like, "What if our industry gets completely deregulated?" and "What if our industry is completely reinvented online?" They articulate new states that may develop and plausible states that capture a range of possibilities; they also consider the joint impact of multiple uncertainties.

One thing that scenario planning can do that contingency planning and stress testing generally do not is consider the interdependence of multiple uncertainties. The other thing that scenario planning does is accurately value and incorporate subjective interpretation. This is why you want the right person writing the scenario.

The advantage to scenario planning is that you are not betting the company on any one of these scenarios. The purpose is to put in place a strategy that is adaptive and resilient enough to cover all of the scenarios. You want to not only survive but sustain and succeed through each of these three, four or five archetypal scenarios. And you want to put in place resilience to cover them all financially, organizationally and culturally to make sure that the strategy that you approved has enough room in it.

Resilience is an engineering term. It means you will bend but not break. No matter how strongly the wind blows, the bridge is not going to collapse. That is your company. That is why you do scenario planning. That is why you do extreme scenarios. Therefore, this is good tool use.

Here are some questions to consider:

How well does our current strategy match the new environment? Do we really want to "go back" to what was normal?

How might we design our plan for resilience? Consider: diversification; built-in redundancy; prudence (stress testing for plausible risks); adaptability; and sense of urgency (versus complacency) — use this time wisely.

How resilient is our strategy?

How confident are we that management understands the changed business model and how this has changed?

Theme 7: Excellence in Crisis Communications

Our next theme is that organizations are getting good at crisis communications. Not that many years ago, when a crisis came up, sometimes the communications became the crisis! Now leaders are really starting to learn how to communicate with simplicity, clarity and effectiveness in a crisis. They are staying focused on key facts, principles and objectives. They are communicating what people need to hear. They are helping people understand why it is that these are the facts, what is behind the facts, what the principles for moving forward are and what the specific objectives of moving forward are. Then, they let others focus on the task, tactics and details.

Some of our political leaders are just exemplary in how great a job they have done in crisis communications. They are communicating consistent messages at a high level, delegating to the next level of government and then looking to the next level for the detail. Those in the next level are playing their roles, staying in the right lane and effectively communicating the messages. Each level is consistent with one another. There are some political leaders that have not reached that level of consistent success.

There are some real lessons here for boards.

As we govern through this, and any crisis, every time the board meets it should be asking these questions:

How well are we doing on crisis communications? Consider: did we play the appropriate roles? Were the delegation of authority and lines of accountability clear, appropriate and respected?

Are there any tweaks, any enhancements that we can or should be making?

Is the board staying on its side of the board/management line?

Are we adding the right value at the right level? (Which likely is just referring people to the CEO.)

How good is our message? How clear is it? How consistent is it? How well is it being received?

Theme 8: Collaboration and Opportunity with Competition

The next theme we are seeing is that there is an unprecedented amount of collaboration with competition. This is happening at both the political and corporate levels. Businesses and governments are collaborating in areas where they have common problems. Yet at the same time, they continue to compete at local and operational levels. Some of your competitors either did not or will not make it. There have been many announcements of both large retailers and small headed for the bankruptcy courts. Others are going to capitalize on this opportunity, and they are going to jump out ahead of you.

A slowed-paced strategy is not intended for times of crisis. Sometimes you might have a strategy in place that serves you well for many years, and then something happens. Everything changes and every moment counts. Your competitors are in crisis mode, just like you are. At times like these, people learn quickly out of necessity. Here are some great questions for you, for your board:

How well is our organization competing at the level of competitive learning and knowledge? Are we keeping up? Are we learning faster than our competition? Are we adapting as a result?

How might we collaborate strategically with competing organizations we share common problems with?

What have we learned about our competition that needs to work its way into our strategic future?

What opportunities can and should we be taking advantage of? Consider, for example, acquisitions – leveraging a strong cash position to take advantage of depressed valuations.

These are significant questions because the competition is going to be even more fierce from now into the foreseeable future. Even though we've had this time of working together collaboratively to solve common crisis-related problems — for example, governments working with governments, banks working with other banks and local businesses working with other local businesses — at the end of the day, there is still that competitive marketplace you are in, and it is going to be fierce.

A tool you want to use here is an E-scan (an external environmental scan). This scan studies your market, your competitors and political, regulatory, economic, social, demographic and technological, factors. How are those factors changing, and how might you expect them to continue to change in the future? And which of these factors can you take advantage of? For example, if you happen to be in a strong cash position and have a good balance sheet, you might be able to take advantage of depressed valuations to move forward with mergers and acquisitions. This allows you to consolidate your organization's market share and your hold on the marketplace. During recession is the time to do that.

What if you do not have a strong position and you do not have a strong balance sheet? What if you are facing a potential insolvency? Part of the board's responsibility is to manage the end of life of this helpless child that we call the corporation. End of life means, rather than waiting for the organization to die a natural and painful death, you might need to step up and negotiate a merger or acquisition sooner rather than later so that you can continue to serve your employees and your suppliers. A really good E-scan will help you with these tough decisions.

Theme 9: Significant Rapid Innovation

Another theme we are seeing that is impacting the board-room is significant, rapid innovation. New attitudes and patterns of demand have emerged during this crisis.

We have talked about some of them already, like the work at home movement and online delivery of products and services. For example, home grocery delivery is flourishing. We hear from people who say that they would be fine to never go into a grocery store again. They want to avoid the crowds and the germs. Another example is online medical services. Both the patient and the clinician are much more willing to embrace technology. We're seeing more takeout and less dining at restaurants, even as they open up. There are more remote meetings and less travel to meetings, and we don't see that changing for some time if ever. This heavily impacts the travel industry. It has been predicted that even two years from now, airline travel won't be at much more than about 60% of pre-COVID travel, 70% at most. Distilleries have pivoted from making beverages to producing cleaning products and hand sanitizer. This leads to another set of questions in your toolkit:

What new attitudes or patterns of demand have emerged through this crisis, and what innovation is this prompting for us?

What innovations are you seeing, and how might they impact your business model?

How might this prompt innovation for your CEO and your organization moving forward?

To recap, here are the top nine themes we are seeing impacting boardrooms:

1. Urgent Pressure to Think Concurrently Through Multiple Timelines

2. A Singular Unique Opportunity to Lead in the Shaping of Culture

3. Cognitive Biases — Especially Pessimism, Optimism and Discounting Biases

4. Multiple Industry Shakeups

5. Compelling Need for Vision Casting to Give People Hope

6. Demand for Adaptability and Resiliency in the Organization

7. Excellence in Crisis Communication

8. Collaboration and Opportunity with Competition

9. Significant Rapid Innovation

We end this chapter with some key questions that we think are important for boards to ask.

Key Questions for Strategic Planning in the New Economy

Theme 1: Urgent Pressure to Think Concurrently Through Multiple Timelines

1. How well is our organization thinking about all four timelines concurrently?
   - o reacting to the crisis (to survive)
   - o recalibrating in the aftershock (to stabilize)
   - o rebounding to the new realities (to sustain)
   - o reimagining the future (to succeed)

Theme 2: A Singular Unique Opportunity to Lead in the Shaping of Culture

1. How aligned, healthy and effective is our organizational culture going forward?
2. How might we use this opportunity to lead in culture formation?

Theme 3: Cognitive Biases — Especially Pessimism, Optimism and Discounting Biases

1. How well have we recognized and challenged any potential cognitive biases that could negatively impact our strategy?
2. How confident are we that our decisions are based on facts rather than a pessimism, optimism or discounting bias?

Theme 4: Multiple Industry Shakeups

1. Which products and services are being delivered by which channel (e.g. in person, online) into which markets? How has this changed? How will it change?

Theme 5: Compelling Need for Vision Casting to Give People Hope

1. To what extent do the vision, mission and values continue to reflect the organization in terms of its horizon point?

2. What is possible?

3. How might we adopt shaping and visionary strategies to influence and exploit the post-crisis landscape?

Theme 6: Demand for Adaptability and Resiliency in the Organization

1. How well does our current strategy match the new environment? Do we really want to "go back" to what was normal?

2. How might we design our plan for resilience? Consider: diversification; built-in redundancy; prudence (stress testing for plausible risks); adaptability; and sense of urgency (versus complacency) — use this time wisely.

3. How resilient is our strategy?

4. How confident are we that management understands the changed business model and how this has changed?

Theme 7: Excellence in Crisis Communications

1. How well are we doing on crisis communications? Consider: did we play the appropriate roles? Were the delegation of authority and lines of accountability clear, appropriate and respected?

2. Are there any tweaks, any enhancements that we can or should be making?

3. Is the board staying on its side of the board/management line?

4. Are we adding the right value at the right level? (Which likely is just referring people to the CEO.)

5. How good is our message? How clear is it? How consistent is it? How well is it being received?

Theme 8: Collaboration and Opportunity with Competition

1. How well is our organization competing at the level of competitive learning and knowledge? Are we keeping up? Are we learning faster than our competition? Are we adapting as a result?

2. How might we collaborate strategically with competing organizations we share common problems with?

3. What have we learned about our competition that needs to work its way into our strategic future?

4. What opportunities can and should we be taking advantage of? Consider, for example, acquisitions – leveraging a strong cash position to take advantage of depressed valuations.

Theme 9: Significant Rapid Innovation

1. What new attitudes or patterns of demand have emerged through this crisis, and what innovation is this prompting for us?

2. What innovations are you seeing, and how might they impact your business model?

3. How might this prompt innovation for your CEO and your organization moving forward?

CHAPTER 2
UNWINDING FROM THE CRISIS —
THE RISKS AND OPPORTUNITY

Risk is not a dirty word!

Risk and opportunity are like two sides of the same coin. We cannot act on an opportunity without taking a risk. And when we take a risk, we do so to act on an opportunity. Risk is not something to fear, nor is it something we need to rid ourselves of. It has long been understood that growth takes risk, and typically the more risk one takes, the higher the potential for returns.

> **Risk and opportunity are like two sides of the same coin.**

Conversely, a risk averse mindset typically leads to lower returns. During a crisis and in a period of an accelerated pace when adaptation and change are needed, the reality is that for many, taking risks is not only needed in order to grow or generate greater returns; risks are necessary for survival.

Especially in a crisis, in order to survive and thrive, your organization may have to undertake more risks than you might be accustomed to or be comfortable with. Risk-taking is more than just introducing a new product or service, entering a new market or approving a large capital spend. It means innovating and reimagining. Maybe your whole business model has been disrupted. Perhaps you need to even reinvent the organization itself. The board has a necessary and valuable role to play here, especially in setting the tone for a healthy risk culture.

The board has three roles in risk governance. The first is risk direction — setting the risk tolerances and appetite of the organization. The board does this in conjunction with management. Management generally holds the pen on these appetites and tolerances. The board and management will agree on the tolerances and appetites that the organization has for risk and the boundaries for both risks and opportunities. In that way, they have jointly set the direction. Both parties have been the rudder of the ship, if you will, for the organization, when it comes to risk.

The second main role that a board has in risk governance has to do with risk oversight. And when we say risk oversight, we mean that it is the responsibility of the board to oversee the effectiveness of the risk management system or ERM, as it is called in many organizations. This role is often completed both by a combination of the board as a whole as well as specific committees of the board. For example, the Audit and Finance Committee may oversee the effectiveness of the financial risk management. The Human Resources Compensation Committee may oversee the effectiveness of human resource and compensation related risks.

The third role that the board has in risk governance is called risk control, which is almost always delegated to the Audit Committee. The purpose of this role is to ensure the organization is "in control" — that the system of controls in the organization are risk-based. This means the accounting and financial disclosure and other governance controls back up, and focus on, the most important or riskier areas of the organization.

Those are the three main areas that we call risk governance. This is the board's role in risk.

It is not uncommon for boards to get caught up in risk management rather than risk oversight. Board members and management alike will benefit from understanding these differences.

It is interesting and yet confusing that there are so many different frameworks for risk governance and risk management. One of the reasons is that risk is a relatively new discipline. Quality and quality management emerged out of Japan in the 1970s, taking the world by storm, with companies large and small adopting the idea that "quality is job one." Quality management went through a series of generations that matured as a discipline. This led to Total Quality Management (TQM), Six Sigma and Leadership, Eliminate Waste, Act Now, Never Ending (LEAN). The latest iteration of quality as a discipline is the embedding of quality into the DNA of the organization, right into every board agenda item and every activity that organizations take.

Corporate governance is similar. Corporate governance started in the 1970s, but it was not really a true discipline until the 1990s. Like TQM and corporate governance disciplines, risk is quite a new field. Risk management started in the 1970s and it started off as a list of potential risks. It has migrated and matured from considering the universe of risk, through enterprise-wide key risks (ERM), to something that is much more performance driven. Modern systems are based on performance-based critical risks aligned with strategy.

Boards are adopting this model of risk governance to optimize risk, fit to the organization. The elementary, operational models tend to focus on financial compliance and operational risks, whereas the fully aligned strategic model looks at strategic performance-based innovation. In the elementary model, there is really no attempt to set a risk appetite or tolerance at the board level. In ERM we start to, but mainly for the risks that are easily quantifiable, like the financial risks at the Audit and Finance Committee level. With integrated strategic risks, we are looking at risk tolerances and appetites being identified for every single type of risk that could significantly affect our objectives both positively and negatively at the board and CEO level, even ones that are not easily quantifiable.

The discipline has gone from long lists to heat maps and traffic lights to adding tools like scenario planning and stress testing. It has moved from being backward looking, to having a past and present focus, to adopting forward-looking integrated risk oversight, where we integrate past, present and future. The main purpose of integrated strategic risk oversight is to look through the windshield of the car to set the direction using forward-focused, leading indicators. For example, we have moved from reacting to managing and to being proactive and continuous. We have moved from avoiding risk to reducing the downside of risk, to mitigation and then to optimization.

We are in the middle of this maturing model, and different boards are at different places in their maturity. The good news is boards and executives are on the risk journey and have matured. They are approaching risk governance and oversight at a much more mature level. This degree of maturity could not have come at a better time.

The rest of this chapter will consider eight questions that will help boards ensure the organization can optimize and maximize upside risks and then manage and set tolerances around the downside risk.

Question 1: How well does the organization's risk culture enable innovation?

As we answer this first question, we will also address a couple of ancillary questions: If the risk culture does not enable innovation, is the culture then acting as a barrier requiring the board's attention from a change management standpoint? And, to what extent is there an over-reaction to failures?

Risk culture, just like any aspect of corporate culture, is a difficult but essential concept for a board to get a handle on. For example, what are the consequences of failure in your organization? The answer to this question is a good indicator of the extent to which your risk culture truly embraces innovation. We try new things to counter the risks, the uncertainties that we face. Sometimes our attempts will work. Sometimes they will not. What happens if an attempt fails? If the answer is that people are punished, demoted, fired, ostracized or red-circled, there is negative punishment attached to failure. You have created a risk culture that is anti-innovation. Not only will this not help the organization welcome innovation, the innovators will leave. They will quietly go away and join other organizations.

Risk culture is a tough thing for the board to get its finger on the pulse of. The main lesson we learned from the 2008 recession is the importance of boards having a handle on risk culture and making sure that the CEO is leading a healthy risk culture.

Sometimes innovation is constantly at the top of management's mind. However, for some, this is not the case. It may be the board that has a higher appetite for risk and innovation than the management team. This prompts our next question.

Question 2: Does your CEO need to be encouraged to incorporate innovation as well as preservation into your risk management framework?

Tiger Woods was once asked, "How did you get to be such a great golfer? You just make it look so easy to be like one of the most naturally great golfers in the world." He responded, "Well, it's easy. All you gotta do is master the things that you're good at but you're not going to change. And then adapt to the things that you do need to change. Then the most important thing is understanding the difference between the two."

In the context of what we're talking about, that means the board and the CEO having a good conversation about what things they should not be changing but making sure they continue to master them. And what things do you need to change? What are the things that you should be adopting and adapting? Which innovations should you be accepting so that you enhance and improve? It sounds easy; of course, it takes hard work. But, like in Tiger Woods' world, that is the secret to success.

Question 3: To what extent does the board receive risk-informed insights?

Our third question drills to the need not just for information but for the right information.

We have a concept called the wisdom mountain, and what the wisdom mountain concept says is that there are all kinds of data in an organization at a raw level. There are millions of bits of data in an organization accessible by board members and executives. But in their raw form they are not very useful. Data need to be rolled up into information to be helpful at a management level. For example, data can be sorted into tables and excel spreadsheets that start to accumulate, group and analyze it.

However, even that is not very helpful at the senior management and board level. You must move higher on the wisdom mountain to knowledge. What does the information teach us? What does it have to do with outcomes? What does it tell us about improving the effectiveness of the organization?

Finally, we reach the pinnacle of the wisdom mountain: applied knowledge. At the boardroom and executive table, the information you are receiving from management and outside advisors should be infused with analysis, interpretation, application and even wisdom.

This is what we mean by risk-informed insights. You want to make sure that the reporting you get from management is not one of those long risk inventory lists. It is not just heat maps and ERM reports. It is a higher level of qualitative forward-looking, interrelated and wisdom-infused information.

Question 4: To what extent does your risk governance framework integrate risk appetite and tolerances?

As we mentioned earlier, the first role of the board in risk governance is setting risk direction, meaning to agree with management on risk "appetite" and "tolerances."

By risk tolerances, we mean the range of acceptable outcomes for each strategic objective. Risk appetite refers to the desirable outcome for a strategic objective.

In both cases, we seek to attach a measure to the degree of risk you are willing to take. The traditional measure of a risk is a combination of severity (impact) and likelihood (probability). These may be in dollars and percentages, but for risks not easily quantifiable, the measure may be on a one to five scale or a similar method.

As management produces risk reports at a higher level of the wisdom mountain, the board can use these reports to ask questions about the most material risks affecting the most significant strategic objectives. A clear, agreed-upon risk governance framework raises the level of dialogue around the boardroom table so that the board can add value at the risk oversight level rather than delving into operational risk management.

Question 5: Does the board have an adequate framework to understand the interrelationships, interdependencies and the compounding effects of risk?

Even organizations with well-crafted risk governance frameworks often neglect to consider the effect of inter-relationships among risks.

In fact, research tells us that the risk events that often prove catastrophic to an organization are usually the result of the incidence of two or more low likelihood but high severity risks, where the incidence of the first risk increases the probability and/or impact of the second, and so on, like a domino effect. In risk parlance, we call this a "perfect storm."

There are different methodologies to incorporate risk interdependencies into your risk governance framework. One of these is clustering related risks in your heat map; you can see the World Economic Forum's Global Risks Map as an example of this. Another is using scenario planning to capture the nuances of multiple events, which is something that a skilled narrator can use to the organization's benefit.

The key, though, is to explicitly acknowledge that inter-dependencies do exist and to include these in your risk governance framework and therefore your dialogue around the boardroom table.

Question 6: How well does your risk governance system consider risk scenarios and stress testing?

Donald Rumsfeld is generally credited with bringing corporate systems thinking into the Pentagon. One of the things Rumsfeld is famous for is his categorization of risk. He said there are three kinds of risks and you deal with each of them differently. There are known known risks, known unknown risks and unknown unknown risks. Known known risks are risks that you understand. You know what they are and how they are going to impact you. The classic tools of ERM work just fine when dealing with known known risks. You can use heat maps, quantifiable risk tolerances, periodic and quarterly reporting.

We will skip over the middle one for a minute. With unknown unknown risks, all you can do is make sure you build enough resilience into the organization to survive them. That means building in things like contingency planning, scenario planning and stress testing. At the end of the day, for these types of risk, make sure you have enough capital and liquidity to get through a crisis.

What about this middle group of risk, the known unknown risk? You know that something damaging could happen. You know it can affect the economy and that will affect your business. The unknown is you do not really know what the specific impacts will be. You have no realistic, reasonable way of measuring them. This is where you use tools like scenario planning and stress testing. That is where they shine. These tools have the capacity to do qualitative analysis of your risks.

Known unknown risk is the type of risk we are facing in the pandemic. These risks are not susceptible to classic tools of quantification, either in the identification, mitigation or monitoring. You want to be using that new set of tools, a newer different set of tools.

Question 7: Do the board's agendas promote integration of risk issues with other agenda items such as strategy, organizational structure and finance?

This is about how you roll out what we have discussed in the first six questions. This is similar to TQM now being embedded in the board's agenda. Unless you are on the board of a hospital or similar organization, you do not see a board agenda topic on TQM. Yet, quality is embedded in most organizations. That is what we are looking at with regards to risk. It is so integrated into your way of thinking it is implicitly and explicitly considered in every agenda item. It is embedded into the DNA of the organization. Every time somebody proposes a program, project, initiative, budget change, reorganization or compensation strategy, the integration of risk and the interdependency of strategic risk are all incorporated. It is part of that maturity model.

Question 8: How confident is the board that emerging risks have been identified in this changing environment?

As you govern through and beyond the current emergency, technology has changed significantly. Whether you are working from home; providing online delivery of education, health or other types of services; maintaining your supplier relationships; attending board meetings or AGMs; or performing other tasks throughout the business model, digital technology has had a disruptive effect. Those are just some examples of areas in which we are now much more exposed to cyber risk and other data driven risks than we were even before the pandemic. It will not belong before our friends in the organized crime world figure out how to take advantage of these opportunities and make some money off them!

This means cyber risk is one example of why you should make sure you are migrating to the highest level of maturity when it comes to risk governance. Are you optimizing risks, including data driven and cyber risks? Are you fitting them to the organization's risk culture and risk profile? Does your board agree with your CEO on risk tolerances and appetite? Risk governance is a not inconsequential tool when it comes to cyber security. Are you using tools like scenario planning and stress testing for your known and unknown risks? Cyber security is almost certainly in that category today, both through and beyond the current emergency. Are you being forward-looking, integrating past, present and future by using well-considered projections? And, are you differentiating between upside and downside risks in your optimization of those risks?

Those are the eight questions in risk direction we think are important for you to ask of yourselves and your management team as you unwind from the crisis.

Key Questions for Unwinding from the Crisis — The Risks and the Opportunities

1. How well does the organization's risk culture enable innovation?

   o If the risk culture does not enable innovation, is the culture then acting as a barrier requiring the board's attention from a change management standpoint?

   o To what extent is there an over-reaction to failures?

2. Does your CEO need to be encouraged to incorporate innovation as well as preservation into your risk management framework?

3. To what extent does the board receive risk-informed insights?

4. To what extent does your risk governance framework integrate risk appetite and tolerances?

5. Does the board have an adequate framework to understand the interrelationships, interdependencies and the compounding effect of risks?

6. How well does your risk governance system consider risk scenarios and stress testing?

7. Do the board's agendas promote integration of risk issues with other agenda items such as strategy, organizational structure and finance?

8. How confident is the board that emerging risks have been identified in this changing environment?

9. For example: What about cyber risk — does the board possess the digital savviness to provide the leadership the company needs?

CHAPTER 3
ATTRACTING AND RETAINING THE BEST EMPLOYEES IN THE NEW ECONOMY

In this chapter, there are seven themes that we will explore related to attracting and retaining the best employees in the new economy:

Theme 1: Strategy

Theme 2: Organizational Values

Theme 3: Succession Planning

Theme 4: Virtual Training

Theme 5: Employee Health and Safety

Theme 6: Engaging People that Work from Home

Theme 7: Compensation Design and Philosophy

Theme 1: Strategy

Here are the questions that your board should be asking in this area:

To what extent will our change in strategies affect our people?

What plans have been put in place to retool or retrain our workforce to enable them to achieve our new/revised strategy?

How confident are you that we can effectively resource these efforts?

It should not surprise anyone that our first theme in the governance level of people oversight is strategy. Everything in governance and operations always comes back to strategy. What you need to excel at depends entirely on what strategies you must pursue and achieve. What you currently are great at may or may not serve you well as you emerge from the pandemic.

We asked our group of 375 board members two more questions. The first one was,

To what extent do you think your organization's goals and objectives will change due to COVID-19?

A full 95% said that they will change to some or a great extent. Looked at another way, only 5% of board members felt their organization's goals and objectives would not change at all.

Then we asked them,

To what extent will strategic changes in the organization change the skill sets required in your senior leadership team?

Based on the answer to the first question, it was no surprise that 69% felt skill sets would need to change either somewhat or significantly!

These are startling and meaningful results.

Most organizations face a lot of changes strategically, and those challenges are going to affect what skills are needed at the senior level. The responses also indicated that some organizations are pivoting entirely. There is only a very small number that were not needing to pivot to some extent or and change skillsets because of the pressure from the pandemic on their business model.

Clearly, organizations are going to have to decide how much energy to put into attracting and changing their workforce rather than retaining and retooling the workforce right from the CEO on down. It is a lot more expensive to attract and change than it is to retrain and retool the workforce.

According to our polls, many organizations will be able to cope with changing human resources skills through retooling and retraining. But a sizable number are going to have to go beyond this and make human resources recruitment a priority.

Boards will want to realize — and ask management questions about — the implications for people direction. The governance system is made up of five levels. The implications for people direction are going to be directly driven by the two levels above it on the governance hierarchy (strategy and risk), and the two levels below (policy and resources).

> We never know what the future holds, but during a pandemic it is foggier than normal.

We never know what the future holds, but during a pandemic it is foggier than normal. Pandemics bring unprecedented risks, both in terms of type and degree. From health and safety to economic and even social order, risk management in the people area shifts beneath our feet.

The policy level, too, is impacted. As more people work from home, and may want to continue to work from home, what policies do you need to put in place to govern this? What expectations do you have of employees and they of you? Even policies such as job descriptions, performance management and compensation design will have to change proportionally to changes in strategy.

Then finally, and not least importantly, is budget. What have these retractions of the economy and workplace health and safety costs done to your financial position and your ability to perform strategically and operationally going forward?

It is really all encompassing how all these things will affect human resources decisions going forward.

Theme 2: Organizational Values

Here are the questions that your board should be asking in this area:

Is our current values statement still valid in the new normal, or do we need to adjust?

What is most important to our people going forward in light of the new social covenant? What changes do we expect?

In what ways will this affect the type of people we hire or rehire?

When we think about strategy, we usually think about goals and objectives and we think about what we should achieve, but a big part of setting strategy is asking what our values are. What are our principles? How do we operate? And our values and principles are tested now more than ever; they're tested during times of crisis more than they ever would be otherwise.

For example, think about the following decision of a large airline: do we refund people who have cancellations due to COVID-19, or do we give them credit vouchers? We would be looking back to our values, and hopefully those values would give us some guidance on what kind of company we want to be, what kind of company we are and where this decision would fit in to that values system.

As a board, ask yourself, is your organization making difficult decisions according to your values? Is your CEO leading people according to your values? Are your employees being treated, and treating others, according to your values?

Further, you will want to reflect on the extent that this pandemic crisis is shifting societal values. Are the values that your significant stakeholders have changing? Your employees, your customers, your members are all looking at life. For many, what's important in life is different today than prior to this pandemic. Things like health and safety, family and work-life balance are coming into play.

Society's values are changing. So, how many organization's values may have to change along with it? You may have to change in order to have healthy and happy employees. To exude the type of company that people want to work for. The type of company that people want to do business with.

A lot of people have compared the current emergency with COVID to wartime. There are many similarities between war and what we're going through here with the current emergency. We are reminded that we saw a significant shift in the social covenant after World War I because women had stepped into the workplace in place of men. And when the war was over, they demanded and won greater rights as a result. Similar shifts happened after World War II.

The suffragette movement, the women's voting movement and women's rights in general were significantly advanced by a forced, not just an unforced, but a forced renegotiation of the social covenant.

We're reminded about civil rights too. The main advances in the civil rights movement in the last century came because men of colour went and died for their country overseas in World War II and in Vietnam. And when the survivors came back, they forced a renegotiation of the social covenant: "If we're good enough to work for you, and we're good enough to fight and die in your place and sacrifice, we're good enough to have the same rights."

We should expect this to happen, especially the deeper and longer this emergency goes on. Boards should be alert to us seeing a global, forced renegotiation of the social covenant. In many countries that generally takes the form of negotiation and compromise, while in other countries, we may see riots in the streets.

In the context of human resources direction and the role of the board, you should be proactively putting out a new social covenant post-pandemic with your employees.

As you contemplate this choice, keep in mind that it costs four or five, even ten times more money every time you have to attract and train a new employee compared with retaining a current employee. And so the more proactive you are in your social covenant, the more benefits you will reap for the organization in human resources.

Theme 3: Succession Planning

Here are the questions that your board should be asking in this area:

Do we have the people resources needed to succeed based on the demands of our new strategies, work environments and reliance on technology?

Is our emergency succession plan ready and clear?

How might the economic and societal changes caused by the pandemic, and our strategic responses to them, affect the desired skills and attributes of the next leader?

Is our succession plan deep enough to withstand potential infection to a large percentage of our senior leadership team?

Are we protecting the senior team from cross contamination?

Succession planning — and the broader task of talent management — is central to attracting and retaining the best employees.

When it comes to succession planning — or any aspect of human resources management — we should distinguish between the board's "parent" and "grandparent" roles. By "parent," we mean the board's direct role in the employment relationship with its one employee, the CEO. By "grandparent," we mean the board's oversight role in the CEOs employment relationships with all the other employees.

During the emergency, most boards have no desire to change CEOs. Having a steady hand at the helm is essential in navigating through the pandemic. And most CEOs are postponing any plans to step down, too, for the time being.

One interesting exception was the Bank of Canada, who decided to continue with their governor's succession during the emergency. This surprised a lot of people, especially given the central bank's role in economic management, but they were already pretty far along the succession process. They kept going, following their pre-set process, narrowed the field to a short list, which included a leading internal candidate, then selected an external candidate. Not a complete outsider, since he was a former deputy governor.

When they brought the new governor in, they were really clear and careful to talk about the handoff and the transition in terms of keeping steady hands at the helm. The main policies were not going to change. They had a good structure in place. They had a good team in place. The current deputy governor was still on the team, and she was the runner up. All of those things were meant to send a signal.

Having said that, if you can avoid doing a planned CEO succession until the emergency is over, probably you should. But if you can't avoid it, then you may need to figure out how to do long-term things like succession. In some ways, then, the Bank of Canada was a reassuring example to us. Maybe that's why they went ahead to say, "You know, we can do this; you can do this." If you've got to do orderly CEO succession, if you can't postpone it, you can do it. You can do it even during a pandemic and come out with a good result.

For most, though, it is emergency CEO succession that is probably going to be top of mind for your board. That means having a clear plan for interim leadership in case your CEO was to leave unexpectedly. This has always been an important board responsibility and is even more so in uncertain times.

This pandemic doesn't necessarily give us any compelling reason to make changes in people, but it does give us a compelling reason to make sure our plan is ready at the level of emergency succession, for no other reason than because your CEO is at a higher risk of catching this deadly virus, as are their natural groomed successor(s). Unpleasant or not, the board needs to think about who would take the CEO's place temporarily. Similarly, as executives return to the workplace, the board will want to be assured that steps are in place to protect the senior team from an outbreak of the virus, which would have a significant impact on the organization, not to mention the human impacts. There's never been a more compelling reason to make sure you've got the first layer of the plan in place.

Longer-term, your board will want to update your CEO succession plan. Once you shift strategy, how do the skills and requirements of the future leader change? Are they still the same as they used to be?

A change in strategy affects the decisions you make about what your leadership is going to look like in the long run. If you're the board of a company like Zoom, or Amazon or an internet delivery service, you're going to be looking for quite a different CEO than the many organizations that are having to innovate and take huge risks to pivot their business model. Their next CEO may be someone who's got to take the reins of a distressed organization and have a different skill set around how to manage people and an organization remotely, perhaps.

Whether you are in thrive mode or survive mode will affect your CEO profile. You will want to make sure that the board is taking these strategy changes into account in CEO succession, just as the CEO is in management succession.

If you're one of those organizations with a major shift in strategy, then you should expect the skills needed of a future leader to be significantly different. If you're facing moderate strategy changes, then it may just mean making some tweaks to having the right CEO profile going forward. Because when we do look at succession, we're looking at the future of the organization. We want the future leadership to be best suited to what we're foreseeing.

Beyond the board's "parent" role with the CEO, the board's role in human resources in general is more of a "grandparent" role. This encompasses human resources beyond the CEO in areas such as compensation philosophy, equity and employee health and safety.

There is always the temptation for boards to roll up their sleeves and get into the kitchen. And especially now, this is even more of a temptation. But, as you sit around the boardroom table, you do want to explicitly differentiate between when you are playing your parent role and when you're playing your grandparent role.

When playing the parent role, that's a conversation you have in a smaller group with the board and the CEO, usually towards the end of the board meeting, without anybody else in the meeting. It's in that in camera session you have just with the CEO, when you're having your conversations about the employment relationship between the board and CEO.

Then there is the broader conversation about the grandparent role, both in regular board meetings, and in much more detail as part of the human resources committee's meetings. Your human resources executive is typically the point person as the responsible manager. You want to be careful when you're filling your grandparent role that you're not directing staff beyond your fact-finding and asking questions and overseeing human resources management. And if you do have some concerns about how the HR executive is managing human resources generally, reserve those for your in camera session with the CEO.

This speaks clearly to the question of talent management, which is all about retaining and promoting the high potential employees in the organization. Your board will want to ask the question of your CEO and your HR executive, to what extent are you identifying the changed skill set in leadership so that you are being successful in talent management?

Unless you have a compelling reason not to, you are almost always far better off to train and upgrade the people you have than to go to the market. It's far more efficient, effective and cost-effective.

The board and its committee responsible for human resources should expect the HR executive and CEO to brief them regularly on succession planning for management. Succession planning starts with needs assessment, and just as with CEO succession, needs assessment is driven directly by strategy. It relates directly to how you see the future of the organization and what skills, character attributes and culture you're looking for in your leadership. This, in turn, creates that profile of attributes you want in the next leader in the next five to ten years.

In terms of the next step in succession, recruitment, the fact that we're in this pandemic and the economy has contracted means millions of people are out of work. And there are some organizations that aren't going to survive. This means that on the recruitment side, in the short term, we see probably the deepest pool of candidates available that there has been in a very long time for all the wrong reasons. And at the end of the day, there are going to be some very good people who find themselves looking for opportunities who normally wouldn't be.

A new challenge affects the next step in succession: selecting an individual. With physical distancing, if you had to go through a transition at this time, how would you do the interviews? How would you select an individual? What processes would you use? What technology would you use? What special considerations does the need for physical distancing bring to selecting an individual where you can't do it the normal way? While many organizations are conducting early rounds of interviews remotely, many have concluded that there is no substitute for in-person meetings to properly get to know and evaluate the top candidates for senior positions.

This same challenge affects the post-selection step: orientation. How do you effectively onboard someone? If you're doing a hiring right now, how do you onboard staff? How do you onboard a CEO? How do you do all that virtually? How do you create a team and perform all of the tasks that you normally would do through close personal interaction?

Clearly, COVID-19 is affecting the entire succession process, and the current situation calls on the board to ask high-level questions of the CEO and HR executive in order to be confident that the succession plan is still on track.

Theme 4: Virtual Training

Here are the questions that your board should be asking in this area:

How well have we transitioned our employee orientation and onboarding to a virtual setting?

To what extent have we designed a virtual onboarding strategy that builds teams and coalesces our employees around our mission?

What plans do we have to provide ongoing professional development that will equip our leadership for the new challenges and opportunities ahead?

The virtual environment is actually an incredible opportunity for us to upgrade your orientation and onboarding program to something much richer than it might have been before.

In the past, orientation for new employees and directors alike was about providing them a pile of documents and expecting them to read them to understand the organization and its strategy.

Instead, because of the need to use technology, you can intentionally sit down opposite a camera and systematically outline your values, your principles, what's important to you. Speak conversationally and use plain language, illustrations, short video clips and interviews with key executives and the chair.

You need to be concise and clear as you seek to induct new members into your team. You need to engage them.

And you may need to continue to engage them remotely if they are working off-site.

Some of the questions you're going to ask as board members are, "How well have we transitioned our employee orientation, onboarding to a virtual setting? Help me to understand how we have designed virtual onboarding? How will we know it's worked?"

The same principles and questions apply to the board's oversight of ongoing training and professional development programs.

Theme 5: Employee Health and Safety

Here are the questions that your board should be asking in this area:

What are our projections and plans for returning to full capacity while protecting our employees' health?

What are the positive and negative impacts to the organization as we adapt our health and safety processes?

What are the long-term impacts to our employees and our customers as social distancing causes us to rethink our employee/customer interfaces?

What have we learned from this pandemic that we can use to adapt?

Part of the board's grandparent role is to evaluate whether they are giving enough direction on risk tolerance and risk appetite when it comes to things like employee health and safety.

When you think about bringing workers back, what should be the board's risk tolerance to management about health and safety? Because you could say that whatever you do, if you bring employees back, none of them can catch COVID-19 in your facility. But that's a very high bar and may not be possible. Or you could say working in your facility should be no more dangerous than being in society. In other words, if we've got community spread of this virus, then working in your facility shouldn't make that worse. Those are two very different risk appetite statements. They're both conveying from a board perspective what your risk tolerance is for the safety of employees coming back to work and different ways of thinking about it. Different organizations are going to take different stances on that. But it's the board's role to set clear expectations on the risk direction side here, after listening carefully to management's recommendations.

Employee health and safety becomes a primary concern of this time. It speaks to what kind of organization you are, how much you care about your employees. Just as we observe in society, the tug between economy and safety will play out within the organization as well.

From a board perspective, the fiduciary duty of a board is to gain reasonable assurance that employees have a safe work environment. Your employees have a legitimate fear of this virus. This really speaks to corporate culture because employee health and safety is an integral part of corporate culture and values. The board's job here is to make sure that that management is not just paying lip service to employee health and safety but really making it a central focus. It needs to be clear that you're not just "greenwashing" this but that you're making whatever changes you need to make, even though those are going to be costly and they're going to cut into your margins, in order to make sure your employees and customers are safe.

You need to be paying equal attention to the health and safety of your employees, your customers and any of your other stakeholder groups, e.g. suppliers, the environment.

You can't tolerate a workplace that is friendly to one and not to another in terms of health and safety.

It's worth mentioning when we talk about employee health and safety, we're not just talking about physical wellbeing but mental health too. And that's under serious strain today. With employees working from home, if they're expected long-term to work from home, you're going to need to invest resources in making sure that you're helping them and giving them the tools they need not just to manage their physical health, if you expect them to come back to the workplace, but to manage their mental health as well if they're expected to continue to work from home.

Boards should have an awareness of and show sensitivity towards women during and beyond COVID, because it has been especially difficult on many women. There's a lot of evidence that many women are being abused more during this crisis than previously. Domestic violence has increased significantly. The shelters are filling up. This is, of course, affecting the workforce and their relationships with their employers. A lot of women are safer when they're going to work, and that's a sensitive and difficult thing to have to deal with. They're going through some really difficult times. This needs to be a part of understanding and helping employees to manage their mental and physical health.

If employees aren't confident they're coming back to a safe workplace, none of your other beyond COVID HR initiatives are going to work.

Theme 6: Engaging People that Work from Home

Here are the questions that your board should be asking in this area:

How might we ensure our values and desired culture are lived out by a remote workforce?

What plans are/will be in place to create an enduring sense of team and belonging in a remote workforce?

How has remote working changed our thinking on the profile of new hires?

What have we learned about our employees' ability to work from home, and how might we leverage that new knowledge going forward?

There's been a shift towards working from home from years, but it's been very slow.

There's lots of evidence that working from home could be more productive and can save companies money. According to some studies, it can save the company up to $11,000 a year per employee, and it can save the employee up to $4,000 a year. And the evidence shows that employees are more productive if they're suited to working from home and if they're supported in working home.

So there are some compelling reasons that the future economy could look very different with fewer requirements for office space if more people are working from home. Indeed, this movement fits nicely into ESG (environmental, social and corporate governance) in that it would be better for the environment with less travel.

After having been forced home due to the lockdown, lots of people are now saying, "You know, I've had to work at home for a couple months. I like it. I'd like to continue doing that." But as a board, you need to understand management's plans for this. How are you going to approach it? How do you engage people when they're at home?

It's not all an ideal "win-win."

Some people and some jobs aren't cut out for working from home. For some, when they are sitting at home working on something and they've got a question for someone, they're probably not going to get an instant answer that they might get in the office. They can't just go around the corner and say, "Hey, I've got a question for you."

Sometimes people can feel isolated. How are you going to manage that? What plans do you have in place to engage them and make sure they're part of a team and part of your culture?

From the board's perspective, it can come down to asking management the question, "How can we gain confidence that we're facilitating and leveraging those employees who are working from home that have a good fit, both job wise and individually?" And then the second piece is, what if a particular job or the employee are not a good fit for remote work? How are you confident that that's even being identified? How might you avoid a permanent drop off in productivity because some people like working from home and don't want to go back to work? In those cases, yet another question that the board needs to ask senior human resources management, through the lens of the grandparent, is, "How can we be confident that those jobs and those individuals are identified and that we therefore have facilitated a return to work?"

Theme 7: Compensation Design and Philosophy

Here are the questions that your board should be asking in this area:

How are we aligning our variable compensation plan to the new priorities and strategic imperatives that we face today?

What, if any, changes will be made to ensure alignment of our employee benefits package to better suit work from home?

You have to be confident as a board that you're giving clear direction to the organization about human resources.

But this direction needs to be at a very high level — one that aligns your human resources plans with your strategic plans and at a level of compensation philosophy and design, not into the weeds.

When it comes to compensation design, there are short-term issues, especially variable compensation.

If you had a variable compensation plan in place, there is a very good chance you didn't hit your targets. This means that boards are going to have to use some discretion on what they do about that with the CEO, and subsequently, what the CEO plans to do with senior leadership incentive compensation (which should be consistent). Right now is a very difficult time to make those decisions; how do you reasonably compensate your CEO and senior leadership team when you're asking them now to work harder than they probably ever have, but you've also got a workforce that's likely sitting at home and maybe not getting paid? There are questions about the equity of that, but also, of the retention and fair treatment of high potential people who may have earned bonuses based on pre-existing agreements.

It's all about fairness at the end of the day. You may be talking about a significant amount of compensation that comes from variable compensation for most CEOs. So it's a big issue.

But aside from incentive compensation, you will also want to look, from a grandparent role, at what your employee benefits are. How does it change the look of what benefits you provide to employees if they're working from home? Is it desirable to work from home so that you may be looking at different benefit packages? Has that created space that now allows you to hire some great employees that may have been available but wanted to work from home? Has this opened to you a workforce that's countrywide or even international versus a small geographic region?

Compensation is a complicated and sensitive subject. In the short term, you just have to decide what the fixes are that need to be put in at an executive level and an employee level to get us through this, but then longer-term, you've got a really big job ahead of you on the HR Committee, with management of course, to look at some redesign of your compensation and benefits plan.

Key Questions for Attracting and Retaining the Best Employees in the New Economy

When the war is over, people want to renegotiate the social covenant. As we come out of sacrifice for the greater good, employees will be looking for a better social covenant, and they will not hesitate to go to employers who will give it to them.

Here are a series of questions boards can ask the CEO to gain reasonable assurance that your organization is positioned for the new normal.

Theme 1: Strategy

1. To what extent will our change in strategies affect our people?

2. What plans have been put in place to retool or retrain our workforce to enable them to achieve our new/revised strategy?

3. How confident are you that we can effectively resource these efforts?

4. To what extent do you think your organization's goals and objectives will change due to COVID-19?

5. To what extent will strategic changes in the organization change the skill sets required in your senior leadership team?

Theme 2: Organizational Values

1. Is our current values statement still valid in the new normal, or do we need to adjust?

2. What is most important to our people going forward in light of the new social covenant? What changes do we expect?

3. In what ways will this affect the type of people we hire or rehire?

Theme 3: Succession Planning

1. Do we have the people resources needed to succeed based on the demands of our new strategies, work environments and reliance on technology?

2. Is our emergency succession plan ready and clear?

3. How might the economic and societal changes caused by the pandemic, and our strategic responses to them, affect the desired skills and attributes of the next leader?

4. Is our succession plan deep enough to withstand potential infection to a large percentage of our senior leadership team?

5. Are we protecting the senior team from cross contamination?

Theme 4: Virtual Training

1. How well have we transitioned our employee orientation and onboarding to a virtual setting?

2. To what extent have we designed a virtual onboarding strategy that builds teams and coalesces our employees around our mission?

3. What plans do we have to provide ongoing professional development that will equip our leadership for the new challenges and opportunities ahead?

Theme 5: Employee Health and Safety

1. What are your projections and plans for returning to full capacity while protecting our employees' health?

2. What are the positive and negative impacts to the organization as we adapt our health and safety processes?

3. What are the long-term impacts to our employees and our customers as social distancing causes us to rethink our employee/customer interfaces?

4. What have we learned from this pandemic that we can use to adapt?

Theme 6: Engaging People that Work from Home

1. How might we ensure our values and desired culture are lived out by a remote workforce?

2. What plans are/will be in place to create an enduring sense of team and belonging in a remote workforce?

3. How has remote working changed our thinking on the profile of new hires?

4. What have we learned about our employees' ability to work from home, and how might we leverage that new knowledge going forward?

Theme 7: Compensation Design and Philosophy

1. How are we aligning our variable compensation plan to the new priorities and strategic imperatives that we face today?

2. What, if any, changes will be made to ensure alignment of our employee benefits package to better suit work from home?

CHAPTER 4

CATCHING UP WITH THE NEW REALITY — RESHAPING POLICIES AND PROTOCOLS

Policy and protocol! I know, this sounds like a bit of a yawner! So much of governance is about the nuts and bolts of governance. That means articulating policies and protocols and gaining reasonable assurance that you're in compliance with them. So, it is a topic we do need to talk about and you need to think about.

The focus of this chapter is on the directional side of policy and protocol. We discuss the compliance and control side in Chapter 7.

There are six overarching themes to consider with respect to the board policy and protocol impacts of governance through and beyond COVID-19:

Theme 1: Virtual Meeting Protocols

Theme 2: Delegation of Authority

Theme 3: Board and Committee Work Plans and Agendas

Theme 4: Code of Conduct and HR Policies

Theme 5: Investment and Risk Policies and Protocols

Theme 6: Policy and Protocol Rollout

While there will be some other policies and protocols to do with business continuity that you will want to think about, we will talk about those later. There may also be some industry or organization specific policies and protocols that only you will know about.

For now, it is your board-level policies we are talking about here. What do we mean by board-level policies? We mean the legal part of your governance system that fits directly underneath the bylaws. Bylaws are typically approved by your membership, although in some instances, approval is done by the board. Bylaws fit underneath the pinnacle of the hierarchy, which is made up of both the act that you're incorporated under and any associated regulations approved by a government. Below the board policy levels are your organization's operating procedures, which are approved by the CEO and staff. The organization may literally have hundreds of those.

The Hierarchy of Governing Documents

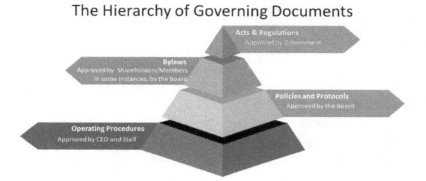

There are usually just a small number of board-level policies and protocols — a dozen, give or take, high-level policies and protocols that are put in place and approved by the board. The purpose of these is to write down in plain language

- the boundaries for the board itself,

- what management is able do between board meetings and

- what management needs to bring back to the board for approval.

In other words, these put the lines and boundaries in place on the road. These give the CEO clarity on where they can and cannot go on the journey that they will travel between board meetings. These documents also give CEOs the confidence they need to know where their lanes are, what they're able to do, how they're able to accomplish it, and before they go over those lines, when they need to come back to the board for input or approval.

That's the purpose of board-level policies and protocols.

The nature of policies and protocols is that they are living documents. These are not carved in stone. The act, and the regulations to a lesser extent, are carved in stone. The bylaws too, which outline the DNA of the governance of the organization, are quite solid. These aren't really expected to change a lot over time. However, board-level policies and protocols are living, breathing documents. They're expected to be reviewed on a regular basis. And in particular, when you are going through any period of change, you should pause and ask, are these policies still relevant and current? Are there some revisions that we should make to them to make sure that we're sending the accurate message to management as to where the lanes are, where the lines in the road are?

It is, therefore, entirely appropriate that at some point in your governance roadmap through and beyond an emergency you will want to review your policies to consider any needed enhancements or revisions. The timing of the review will depend on the extent to which your organization has been affected. This book provides a roadmap of steps you will need to take and questions you will want to consider. It is not intended to be a calendar. You will need to attach your own best timing to this process. In some of your organizations, this roadmap could cover several months — likely in the neighbourhood of six months. You will want to ask yourself when an appropriate time for the board would be to review cross cutting, board-level policies and protocols and then schedule it as part of the post-crisis roadmap you're putting in place.

Theme 1: Virtual Meeting Protocols

Now that we are well into the holding virtual board and committee meetings, and even annual general meetings (AGMs), boards have learned and settled on the technology platforms they will use for meetings and voting. People have become comfortable with the technology.

What many have not done is made sure they have approved protocols for virtual meetings. Organizations have all found ways to meet online, but many did not check to see if their rules even allowed for it! In many jurisdictions, governments needed to approve the use of technology to hold virtual AGMs. For others, bylaws needed to be changed to allow for it. For others, board-level policies and protocols either needed to be created or revised.

Your first two questions then are these:

Can we legally hold a virtual meeting?

Can we hold a virtual AGM, or do we to postpone it, either until we can meet in person or until we can get the needed approvals in place?

Our perspective is not to wait to either meet as a board or to hold your AGM. If you continue to wait until you can gather large groups of people in person, you're putting at risk the flow of your annual governance. That means, the renewal of your board, orientation of board members, refreshing of committees and officers (including board and committee chairs) and even the work plans of the board and committees are all getting moved forward into the coming year. At a time when you need to be adaptive and resilient, you need to keep things moving, not slow them down. It will not help you in the long term if you truncate your year.

The third question is this:

Are our policies and protocols updated to reflect our new practices?

You may have already adopted a Virtual Meeting Policy. However, even if you adopted one back in February or March, you may not want to customize it based on your experience over the last meeting cycle or two. Things are changing, and we are learning rapidly about what works, what doesn't and what to watch out for.

At the end of this chapter, you will find a sample Virtual Meeting Policy that you may use and adapt to fit your own organization and situation.

Theme 2: Delegation of Authority

In a crisis, boards often move the line — that bright red line that exists between the board and management. It has been no different with the COVID 19 crisis. Some have moved it; others haven't. For those who have moved down into operations, we encourage you to redraw it in its traditional place. Post-crisis, the board should get back to governing. They should not be intervening or even assisting management in the operations of the organization. Recently, we interviewed several CEOs and asked them, "What do you need from your board right now?" and, "To what extent has the line between the board and CEO moved through this crisis, and where would you expect it to settle out post-crisis?"

The consensus was that the knee-jerk reaction was for boards to want to get involved in the day-to-day, to meet more often and expect more time with the CEO. This was not ill-intended. They just wanted to help. However, what the CEOs really needed was to not have the board in the day-to-day, to meet less frequently and to free up their time so that they could lead their team through the crisis!

These CEOs appreciated their boards and the boards' good intentions. But they were already under so much pressure to keep things on course and manage the crisis, what they really needed was for the board to stay in their governance lane. They did recognize the need for frequent, clear, communications on what was going on inside the organization. They knew they needed to make sure their board was fully apprised of the risks were they dealing with, how these risks were being mitigated and what the board needed to be aware of. Brief, frequent conversations with the chair and weekly updates for the board under the circumstances may have been warranted. As one CEO said to us, "I meet with my board on a weekly basis, just for a catch up and to let them know where things are at or if I need anything from them. The key is 'no surprises.' But it's more of a sharing mechanism rather than a telling mechanism. And it's brief."

A good board will want to assist the CEO though all types of unexpected events, and a good CEO would want that advice and dialogue with the board. There's a natural inclination when there is a crisis, as a board, or even as a leadership team, to want to be able to have impact and to influence the decisions that are being made. But they should both stay safely in their lanes rather than get too close to the centre lane and let the line become blurred.

There are three questions that we propose you consider related to delegation of authority. The first is this:

How has the line between the board and CEO changed since the emergency?

You should ask that question even if you don't think the line has changed because maybe the perception on the other side of the boardroom table is different than your own. How is the current level of board interaction landing on the CEO? You may not have intentionally moved the line, but the CEO might feel like it has moved.

The second question is this:

How would we expect the line to be drawn long-term post-emergency?

In some cases, that will mean figuring out how to revert to a governing-type board rather than one that has become intervening. What are the intentional steps you will need to take to revert to a normal, governing board? The reason that's a challenging question is because it's much easier to move down the governance spectrum than up. It's much easier to call more frequent meetings and get closer into the kitchen than it is to call less frequent meetings and to get out of the kitchen. You will want to put a roadmap in place to make sure that that happens.

The third question is this:

How well does our delegation of authorities reflect our new practices?

The delegation of authority is probably one of the two most important board-level policies in most organizations. Are there some changes you need to make to it right now? Are there some changes you need to make as you come through the emergency? Are there certain types of decisions that haven't been captured in your delegation of authorities until now? It is possible that the delegation of authority revision might be to expand it, to delegate more authority to your CEO, to touch on areas that you hadn't previously considered?

The reality is, we'll never be back at normal, whether it's from a business standpoint, a market standpoint or indeed even a governance standpoint. So, it's important to be able to reset. There's an understanding and a sympathy for wanting to be able to get more involved in the operational details, but there needs to be a resetting. Rather than substituting your judgment for that of the CEO's, make sure that you have a good delegation of authority policy, as that's the tool that you use.

In the COVID crises, we are seeing organizations being impacted across the spectrum. For some, this is a tremendous crisis. It has affected their business from top to bottom. For other businesses, it's been business as usual. Still other businesses have experienced tremendous growth. Which one of the scenarios you find yourself in will reflect where your line between the board and CEO gets drawn and reset.

Theme 3: Board and Committee Workplans and Agendas

Boards and committees are highly focused on those issues that are both urgent and important. Naturally, we would expect to see that at a time like this, but as a result, both the less urgent but also important matters are being postponed.

This raises questions about how to reorganize and optimize the work plans of the boards and committees.

Here are some questions that you may want to consider as you begin a new governance year:

As we begin a new governance year, what needs to be on the board's work plan?

o   *What needs to be on the board committee work plans?*

Are we doing the right things?

o   *What did we start doing that we need to stop doing?*

o   *What did we stop doing that we need to start doing?*

o   *What did we stop doing that we need to continue to stop doing?*

Have board and committee charters been updated

to ensure currency?

What we've observed since the beginning of COVID, in the first cycle of board and committee meetings, is that most board committees did not meet, or they met as a committee of the whole. Now that we are beyond the initial shock to our corporate systems, committees have begun to resume their meeting schedules; however, they have trimmed and streamlined their agendas. They are laser focused on the most substantive matters. To some extent, this has been quite therapeutic because it's caused board members to ask the question, "Are there some things that had crept onto our agendas that we should not have been doing in the first place? In fact, maybe some of those things were not even in our terms of reference to begin with!" They are learning that many items on their agendas can be dealt with consent agenda or information items. They are also recognizing that many items are operational enough that they should be delegated to management.

This is a good time to refresh the work plan of your committees. Consider what you stopped doing that you probably can continue to stop. Then, what did you stop doing that you need to restart? Then, what did you start doing that you may need to stop? What are some things that you did because of the emergency or the crisis that were transitional? They are things that don't need to be on the long-term work plan of the board or committee. The general sense is that this is a good opportunity for those of us going through the annual refreshing of the committees and the committee chairs to do that now in this window.

An example of this might be boards that started meeting weekly for information updates. That's something that you've started that you will want to stop. An example of something that you stopped that you may need to start is your annual board evaluation or CEO evaluation. Many boards postponed this part of their annual cycle. These are now out of sync with the business cycle. You need to pick those up and plan for how you'll restart those things. Then of course, the operational activities that may have crept onto the board's agenda in the height of the crisis need to be stopped.

Theme 4: Code of Conduct and HR Policies

This is certainly the area where we are seeing lots of potential policy implications.

Here is what you should be thinking about in this area:

Have our Code of Conduct and broader HR policies been updated to consider

- *physical distancing effects on aspects of conduct?*

- *confidentiality: securing electronic communications and materials?*

- *working from home?*

- *harassment, abuse, respect, "whistle-blowing" (integrity assurance)?*

This is a complex area. Every organization will have differing and nuanced answers to these questions. We will pose the questions and leave them for you to take back to your executive team. It would be a good idea to send the questions to them before the meeting so that they can prepare answers! That's probably something that they'd appreciate.

Earlier we said that the delegation of authorities is generally one of the two most important board-level policies. The other is the Code of Conduct. If you have a really strong, robust delegation of authority and the CEO has a clear understanding of that delegation, and if you've got a really good Code of Conduct, everybody knows what behaviours are expected of them.

These should be living, breathing documents. It's time to refresh them and make sure you are all familiar with them. There are two main drivers of your Code of Conduct and your HR related policies.

The simpler driver is employees, customers and suppliers returning to the workplace. You have some questions to ask that we touched in the previous chapter about safety, physical distancing and how the workplace provides a safe yet an effective work environment. Do your employees feel comfortable and confident going into the workplace? Do your customers, suppliers and others feel safe? It's going to call for resourcing. It's going to cost money. You will want to make sure that the board understands the importance of resourcing that level of safety.

The second main driver is for employees who are not returning to the workplace but being asked to work from home. This can be quite complicated. You're talking about property that belongs to the company that's off premises. How do you secure that? How do you ensure confidentiality? How do you secure retention and destruction of sensitive, commercial material?

In record time, organizations have had to resource employees in terms of not just a hardware but internet broadband and in-home office equipment and furnishings. In addition to these more practical and visible features of conduct and HR policy for the home workplace, there are significant impacts to employee mental health and physical safety at home.

Home is not always the safest place for people. In fact, for many, home is sometimes an unsafe place, and it can be quite challenging for them to admit that or to reach out if they need support. The board wants to make sure that your HR staff are being proactive and assertive in assuring there are supports and resources available to your employees in case there's abuse or harassment at home. And then there is also the whole broader area of mental health beyond specific instances of abuse.

Theme 5: Investment and Risk Policies and Protocols

We talked about risk in Chapter 2, but here we want to spend some time on the policy side of risk. Similarly, with the volatility and drops in capital market values, it may be prudent and timely to review your Investment Policy. And so we pose these two questions:

What are the implications for our Investment Policy, and has the policy been updated?

What are the implications for our Risk Oversight Protocol, and are these reflected adequately in our protocol?

These are two of the dozen or so board-level policies that we see in most organizations. And these two in particular have been directly affected by the volatile swings and uncertainties in the capital markets and in the broader risk environment. Usually, these are situated with the Audit and Finance Committee. Certainly, the Investment Policy is. Depending on your committee structure, your Risk Oversight Protocol could either be situated at the board level (preferably), with the Audit and Finance Committee or, if you have a Risk Committee, with it. A review and refresh of this protocol should be on your radar. You don't want to have an Investment Policy or Risk Protocol that no longer fits the current capital market and risk environment.

Theme 6: Policy and Protocol Rollout

Policies and protocols are just a reflection of what the board and management teams have agreed on together. However, they're just words on a page if they're not written in the hearts and the minds of the people being asked to live out these documents. That's why we've posed these last two questions:

How confident are you that there is buy-in to and understanding of these new policies and protocols?

Are the implications of any new policies and protocols in need of resourcing, and if so, are those resources in place?

What we're talking about is how to get these from the paper into people's minds and into their hearts. This is even more challenging of course when people are remote and when we're still learning about virtual professional development, training, employee orientation, updating existing employees on changes and breathing life into these changes.

Many Codes of Conduct sound a little bit like the Ten Commandments: thou shall not do this, shall not do that, thou shall not do the other thing. Codes of Conduct are better written as covenants. For example, "Here's what you can expect from us, and in return, here is what we expect from you." They also include real-life examples of the types of dilemmas that you might find yourself in ethically. This is really helpful when it comes to a Code of Conduct. This is just an example of how otherwise dry policies — these words on a piece of paper that are intended to be the lane markers for the road forward — can be made practical, relevant and interesting. You want people to read them and say, "Oh yeah. Okay. I get that. Oh, now I see what you're saying." Organizations will need to learn how to pass along the meaning of policies to employees, even though they can't do it in person. Perhaps, they could do it even better than they do have in the past!

Boards are famous for approving strategies and policies and then forgetting about resourcing them and hoping that staff will just figure out how they're going to it done. It's easy to pass a resolution that gives the CEO five more things that they want done by the next board meeting! The board has an obligation to not just to pass motions but to make sure that resources are carved: financial, human, technical and other tangible resources to support the policies that you put in place. In our next chapter, we will discuss refreshing the financials and projecting what comes next.

Those are our six themes in this chapter on reshaping board-level policies and protocol post-COVID:

1. Virtual Meeting Protocols

2. Delegation of Authority

3. Board and Committee Work Plans and Agendas

4. Code of Conduct and HR Policies

5. Investment and Risk Policies and Protocols

6. Policy and Protocol Rollout

Remember, in difficult times, it's easy for a board to slip into more meetings and redraw the line between the CEO and board toward being more operational. You will want to counteract that intentionally when you do your policy review. Don't wait until you're all the way through and COVID is fully in the rear-view mirror. If you can, start the reset now!

Key Questions for Catching Up with the New Reality — Reshaping Policies and Protocols

Here are a series of questions boards can ask the CEO to gain reasonable assurance that your organization has reshaped its policies and protocols to fit the new reality.

Theme 1: Virtual Meeting Protocols

1. Can we legally hold a virtual meeting?

2. Can we hold a virtual AGM, or do we postpone it, either until we can meet in person or until we can get the needed approvals in place?

3. Are our policies and protocols updated to reflect our new practices?

Theme 2: Delegation of Authority

1. How has the line between the board and CEO changed since the emergency?

2. How would we expect the line to be drawn long-term, post-emergency?

3. How well does our delegation of authorities reflect our new practices?

Theme 3: Board and Committee Work Plans and Agendas

1. As we begin a new governance year, what needs to be on the board's work plan?

   o What needs to be on the board committee work plans?

2. Are we doing the right things?

   o What did we start doing that we need to stop doing?

   o What did we stop doing that we need to start doing?

   o What did we stop doing that we need to continue to stop doing?

3. Have board and committee charters been updated to ensure currency?

Theme 4: Code of Conduct and HR Policies

1. Have our Code of Conduct and broader HR policies been updated to consider the following?

   o physical distancing effects on aspects of conduct

   o confidentiality: securing electronic communications and materials

   o working from home

   o harassment, abuse, respect, "whistle-blowing" (integrity assurance)

Theme 5: Investment and Risk Policies and Protocols

1. What are the implications for our Investment Policy, and has the policy been updated?

2. What are the implications for our Risk Oversight Protocol, and are these reflected adequately in our protocol?

Theme 6: Policy and Protocol Rollout

1. How confident are you that there is buy-in to and understanding of these new policies and protocols?

2. Are the implications of any new policies and protocols in need of resourcing, and if so, are those resources in place?

Sample Virtual Meeting Policy

Virtual Meeting Policy

Principle

The need for and advantages to holding electronic and virtual meetings from time to time are both acknowledged and necessary. This policy is intended to provide guidance for organizations when holding and participating in these meetings.

Policy

This policy provides for the use of electronic means for the holding of meetings of the members, board, and committees of a board, including a committee of the whole board.

Virtual, electronic meetings may be used to hold member, board or committee meetings subject to due notice requirements for any such meeting being met (or waived by unanimous consent in special circumstances).

All participants must have access to the necessary equipment for participation. A right of membership is participation; therefore, the technology used must be accessible to all members who are to be included in the meeting.

All rules pertaining to in-person member, board or committee meetings apply equally to virtual, electronic meetings, for example, notice, pre-meeting package requirements, quorum, minute taking, voting, confidentiality requirements, etc.

All meeting participants must ensure they maintain complete privacy in their off-site meeting space. This will ensure all discussions are kept confidential and are only heard by those invited to and attending the meeting.

All provisions and policy related to in camera meetings and conflict of interest will apply equally for virtual, electronic meetings of the members, board or committees.

At no time will meeting participants record any portion of the meeting. The only exception to this is any recording made by the corporate secretary or other approved corporate officer for the purpose of minute taking. Any such recording must be destroyed once the official minutes of the meeting have been approved.

In no circumstance are discussions in the "chat" function of virtual meeting software to be copied and saved by meeting participants or included as part of the official meeting minutes.

Subject to any conditions or limitations provided for under the act, regulations, bylaws or this policy (which some jurisdictions waive during the course of a declared emergency), a member, board or committee member who participates in a meeting through electronic means shall be deemed to be present at the meeting and will be recorded as in attendance at and part of the quorum of the meeting.

Virtual Meeting Procedure

- The chair of the board or committee will be the chair of the meeting.

- Any technology employed will enable every participant to hear and be heard by all other participants in the meeting.

- The chair will ensure that declarations of conflict of interest are heard by all present and that those participating have an opportunity to verbally declare any conflict.

- The meeting will be administered in such a way that the rules governing conflict of interest are complied with.

- The electronic means will enable appropriate processes to ensure the security and confidentiality of proceedings, both regular and in camera meetings. This may mean using separate connections and log-ins for scheduled in camera/executive sessions.

- Attendance shall be taken and duly recorded to ensure participants are recognized as in attendance.

- Participants will identify themselves before speaking in order to assist the recording secretary in recording the minutes.

- Those participating in a virtual, electronic meeting shall notify the chair of their departure (either temporary or permanent) from the meeting before absenting themselves in order to ensure a quorum is maintained.

- All meeting participants must have a copy of the meeting package, including the agenda, prior to the meeting for reference during the meeting.

- Wherever possible, motions coming forward at the meeting should be prepared ahead of the meeting with one of the eligible members indicating their willingness to let their name stand as mover and another as seconder. Prior to the vote, the chair will read each motion and indicate the member who is moving and seconding the motion.

- Voting at virtual, electronic meetings shall be carried out as follows to ensure that accurate records of votes are maintained:

    o   When a vote is called, opposition to the motion is called first.

    o   If no one is opposed, the motion is considered carried.

    o   If there is opposition, a roll call vote is held, and the chair will announce the number of votes cast in favour or against the motion and whether the motion is carried.

    o   The chair will make the decision as to whether the motion was carried or defeated.

    o   When the technology does not allow for those votes requiring a secret ballot, a confidential email should be in place between meeting participants and the scrutineer to facilitate secret votes.

- To avoid as much disruption as possible and to support seamless dialogue and debate, all participants will keep their electronic devices on mute unless speaking.

- Any open chat windows in the technology must be used only to resolve technological problems. They should not be used for side discussions, lobbying other members and participants or voicing support for motions on the floor. Members, boards and committees meet and have authority only as a collective with due order.

Review: Annually by Governance and Nominating Committee

CHAPTER 5

REFRESHING THE FINANCIALS AND PROJECTING WHAT COMES NEXT

In this chapter and the next, we're going to be talking about the financial aspects of governance and oversight. We're looking at the directional side in this chapter, and next, we're going to be looking more at the control side of financial oversight. In both cases, we'll explore some of the implications related to COVID-19 and getting through and beyond it.

There are five themes we'll consider related to the financial impacts of governance:

Theme 1: Revenues

Theme 2: Expenses

Theme 3: Cash Flow

Theme 4: Bridging the Gap

Theme 5: Refreshing the Budget

Experience tells us that the overarching theme of financial direction is cash. It's about making sure that your organization survives through and beyond the current crisis.

There is a saying, "Cash is king." That's because research shows us that the number one cause of business failure, not just in a recession but in a time of growth too, is running out of cash — a liquidity crunch.

Therefore, the overarching question that we'll unpack in several different layers has to do with how confident you are that you have enough cash for the next 30, 60, 90 days and beyond. Whether it's your board or your Audit Committee dealing with financial and risk oversight, each is on high alert. This is because there's a range of urgent issues and volatility that are causing management to constantly adjust and update your financial projections and forecasts. You're probably faced with a shifting liquidity and risk environment.

Within this imperative, to retain enough net cash, are two frames. First comes the short-term updating of financial projections to make sure you've got enough cash flow to survive, to keep the doors open. And then longer-term: at what point do you establish a realistic operating and financing plan that allows you to come out of the other end of the economic downturn?

Theme 1: Revenues

Pragmatically, there are only a limited number of ways to generate cash flow: from operating, financing and investing.

For those of you familiar with the financial statements, you'll probably recognize that what we're doing here is going through your Statement of Cash Flows in the exact order they appear there. We're always looking for a comprehensive way to attack a subject. Your Statement of Cash Flows is that one page in your financials that summarizes your sources and uses of cash. We'll start with the revenues and expenses and the net cash flow generated from operations.

First, operating. Again, to quote a well-worn phrase, there are only two ways to generate more income: "You can cut expenses, or you can grow revenues."

When we're in a downturn, the natural inclination to start is by looking at ways to cut expenses. Before making those cuts, your board's key question on the revenue side should be this:

How confident are we that we have optimized opportunities to increase revenues?

We recall a young, inexperienced CEO who, when hit with a recessionary period, immediately focused on cutting expenses, which essentially meant cutting jobs. That was their number one variable or discretionary expense. It started them on a downward spiral in asset and revenue shrinkage that ended only with a merger with a larger entity. And only in hindsight did that CEO realize that they should have started by focusing on growing revenues, on exploring opportunities to replace and grow their revenues, of which there were many.

In hindsight, they understood that they could have easily expanded into other markets that were underserved at the time and that all would have benefitted from. Had they done that, they would have saved more jobs and been a more viable and sustainable organization going forward.

We've talked in earlier chapters about how many businesses are finding innovative opportunities in this crisis. They're generating revenues from the sale of products and services online. For many, the pandemic has a silver lining— an opportunity to innovate your product-market mix.

What products and services are already in your arsenal that you can deliver online? What new products and services can you design to generate sales? There are the examples of a distillery making hand sanitizer, of a clothing maker making PPE, of an auto parts manufacturer making ventilators. You may not need to make such dramatic changes to your product mix. This market is rewarding innovators, entrepreneurs, risk-takers.

Look at your marketplace. What small shifts in target markets would enable you to sell online or to move to a delivery or pick-up model? How can you reach these new customers? How can you optimize your social media and digital marketing presence?

As the weeks of the pandemic have ground into months, marketplaces are settling down, people are finding a way to live their lives without unduly going out of their homes. These shifts have generated tremendous opportunities for a wide range of sectors, including for-profit and not-for-profit. Most sectors are seeing a return close to earlier, pre-pandemic levels of revenue.

There are other opportunities too; some are looking to government emergency assistance programs, special business loans and business interruption insurance.

Theme 2: Expenses

Once you've fully exhausted your revenue generating options, you can turn to the expense management side. Here, your board's overarching question is,

How confident are we that we have optimized opportunities to reduce expenses?

Of course, when it comes to operations, every organization is unique. Your own business model is going to dictate where you can look for opportunities to grow revenues and to cut expenses.

Generally, when we look at expenses, we look at discretionary items. In other words, what are items that you don't have a contractual obligation to complete? What are some areas where you have an opportunity to trim?

Dividends are discretionary. And they're one of the first things that we cut if we're not generating good net income. Our shareholders should not be surprised if we're going to reduce or even pause our dividend payments for a time.

Another very common example that we're seeing, of course, are layoffs and furloughs of employees. In the case of most clients and organizations that we see, they're really thinking this through and thinking about a long-term plan. How can you achieve talent management and attract and retain high potential employees while at the same time rebalancing your payroll expenses to match your levels of revenues more closely? We have good research data that says that it costs about four to ten times multiplier for every employee you need to replace versus an employee that you can retain.

In some cases, this has led to work-sharing with reduced hours rather than layoffs or lower wages. The government's emergency wage subsidy program has been used by many to spare employees' job cuts and to retain strong staff who will be needed when the markets tighten up again. But for some, such as in the travel and hospitality sectors, job cuts are the only plausible alternative.

Another opportunity to cut costs is with bonuses and incentive compensation. We're seeing many organizations deferring those. Some organizations are substituting share payments in lieu of cash for executives and board members. We should caution you that this could have an unintended backlash effect if there's a windfall later. If you issue shares now at the very low point of your shares as a way of saving cash, that seems legitimate because you want to save cash and you want to send a signal to people that you're taking a hit too at the executive and directorship level. But, what if a year from now, there's a huge windfall that these people have made? You're going to hear back about that. So again, think through the unintended consequences of every action that you take. Like Newton's law states, there's an equal and opposite reaction for every action.

We're seeing some organizations instituting cuts in pay for leadership. We're seeing CEOs and C-suite executives taking 5%, 10%, 20% cuts in pay. We're seeing board members doing the same — pausing or reducing compensation that is symbolic, but it's not unimportant. It's sending a message to employees that you're sharing the pain of the reduced revenues when it comes to cutting discretionary expenses.

Both perception and fairness are principles for the board to weigh when it comes to paying the CEO, be it their base salary or incentive compensation. CEOs have been working around the clock to reinvent the business model and save their companies, and so many have earned their compensation and more, but it is difficult to do this while laying off other employees.

Cutting costs for facilities is another option. If the bulk of your workforce is working from home, are you able to reduce the rent that you are paying for workplaces?

Both staff and premises have related ancillary expenses that you should be able to save correspondingly, like training, travel, office supplies and utilities.

You may have opportunities to save money in other areas of operating expenses, such as marketing, insurance, banking and professional services. Collectively, these can take you a long way to balancing your cash flow, to stemming the bleeding.

We share these examples to stimulate your thinking. Of course, this is management's job anyway — to come up with these ideas. The board's job is to gain confidence that management has done its job in exercising good judgment and optimizing opportunities to increase revenues and reduce expenses.

And while you weigh the benefits to cutting discretionary costs, you will want to weigh reputational and other potential costs. There is always a trade off: every time you cut an expense, there are consequences, both direct and potentially indirect. You want to make sure that as you cut expenses, you're crafting messages to the stakeholder groups that are affected by them to make sure they understand the context you were faced with when cutting expenses.

Keep in mind, you're going to have some upward pressure on expenses at the same time, too. Don't be surprised to see, when your Audit Committee gets your next set of financial projections from management, that some of the line items are actually going up, not down. For example, it's going to cost money to resource the emergency, to fund changes to the workplace in order to turn them into safe places for employees and customers. Also, there are potentially one-time costs equipping employees that are going to be working from home. There are training expenses, and there are all kinds of one-time costs associated with dealing with the emergency and the crisis right across the board.

It's a balancing act when it comes to operations. Do what you can to grow revenues in innovative ways. Do what you need to do to cut expenses. And don't forget that there are also going to be additional commitments and expenses that you might not have planned for.

Theme 3: Cash Flow

Beyond operating cash flow, what other areas are there where you could be generating cash flow quickly to offset that drop in revenues? We're going to look at working capital management and then financing and investment opportunities.

Our next three questions are related to working capital management:

How confident are we that we have enough cash for the next 30, 60, 90 days and beyond?

How confident are we that we have enough cash to weather the storm for the long haul?

How confident are we that we are optimizing our cash flow through working capital management?

Optimizing our cash flow through working capital management means that there may be areas where you may not be able to grow revenues, but you might be able to speed up the cash flow from them. There may be areas where you can't cut expenses, but you could slow down the cash flow from those expenses.

One example that affects us directly is businesses not refunding payments even though they cancelled delivering the product or service. In our organization, we have quite a large credit with our airline for those March and April flights that had been booked and then cancelled because of the lockdown. In financial accounting terms, this is called deferred revenue. It's a liability on the airline's balance sheet because they still owe either the money or the service. The last thing the airline wants to do when it's already laying off 80% of its employees and flying planes with almost no one on them is to write a bunch of cheques to refund people for all the flights that were cancelled.

The relevant questions for you here are, do you have deferred revenue in your organization? Are there timing differences in the delivery of your goods and services versus cashflow, and how might you optimize that?

Another related area to look at is your trade creditor relationships and your payables. We call this "leaning on the trade." Essentially, what it means is you renegotiate your credit terms with your suppliers in exchange for continuing to do business with them and making them preferred suppliers — in some cases, maybe even an exchange for paying higher prices or whatever you negotiate. Your suppliers might agree to more generous credit terms so that you can use them essentially as a provider of capital to the organization and not have to have that cash flow leave your organization so soon.

You will want to manage the supplier relationship, making sure you've got a supplier — a good supplier, a continuity and not an over-reliance on suppliers that might go out of business themselves.

On the asset side of the balance sheet, you want to look at the same thing in terms of receivables. What's the collectability of your receivables? Left alone, they're probably going to slow down; 30 days become 60 days, and 60 days become 90 days. What can you do about that proactively to engage with those clients, to essentially enter a relationship with them that they're paying you and you're continuing to do business with them?

Another aspect of working capital is inventory. If you're in the retail or the manufacturing business, you could have a lot of inventory on hand right now. What's the saleability, what's its true value in today's marketplace? Does it shrink in value over time? Are there things that you can do with it? Can you put it on consignment? Can you cut its price and sell it?

If you think about the financial institution business, the product that you have is money. You can price that money on the two different sides of your balance sheet depending on supply and demand. If you're looking to raise deposits for example, which is one way we build up cash flow, one of the ways that you can do that is by increasing what you pay for those deposits — the interest rates and the terms that you pay on deposits. And the flip side is in dealing with loans. By offering lower interest rates on loans, you will have higher loan demand and cash outflow.

These are examples of tools that you can use in working capital management. Keep in mind, this is management's job. We're not inviting the board to get into the kitchen and start getting into the details of working capital management, but you'll want to be familiar with what some of these tools are. We would suggest you pull out your Statement of Cash Flows and just go through it line item by line item and have that conversation between the Audit Committee and the CFO in terms, asking them if they are optimizing the cashflow in these areas.

Theme 4: Bridging the Gap

Our fourth theme has to do with "bridging the gap." What if the combination of operating and working capital management is not enough to generate enough cash flow to keep you going? What other avenues are there?

And that leads us to these next two questions:

How might we bridge the gap?

To what extent do we need to consider a sale of your assets?

At the end of the day, if you haven't balanced your cash flow, you may need to lean back on financing and investing alternatives. Financing has to do with the liability side of your balance sheet beyond current liabilities, and investing has to do with the asset side of your balance sheet beyond immediate working capital.

Let's look at financing first. What are some liability-driven solutions here? One obvious example is you could borrow more money. That's why operating lines of credit exist in the first place. That's why committed lines of credit from your central lender are in place. When there's a rainy day, when you have a need of cash for working capital, you can draw on your operating line of credit.

You will certainly want to sit down with your main lender and have a good conversation with them about your strategy regarding cash flow management so that they're comfortable with that. Alongside that, they may suggest restructuring debts. When we go through difficult times in any sector, it may make sense to restructure debts, maybe to postpone short-term payments, maybe to convert short-term to long-term debt, maybe converting debt to equity.

But even that may not be enough or sustainable; you might need to go deeper.

Another option is to raise new capital. It's been surprising to see the large volumes of money raised on capital markets by new equity issues since the pandemic began. If you have a small number or even one cash-rich investor, if you're a privately-held company, this may well be a time to restructure your shareholding so that you get a big cash injection from an investor to keep you going through this time.

Another financing option may be to use your reserves if you have set aside surplus earnings from previous years for a rainy day. Management may propose tapping into reserves as part of a discussion with the board about a COVID survival strategy.

Shareholder loans or advances are a way to bridge the gap in operations that don't require you to rely on a lender. And in fact, your lender may require shareholders to kick in a proportion of the contributions on the liability side of your financing before they commit new money.

If you're a not-for-profit, you may have major benefactors who have helped you out in the past in difficult times. They may be able to see you through this tough period.

Turning to the asset side, what we call investing, is there a possibility to sell assets? Do you have assets you can sell to generate one-time cash flow? These may be assets that you're holding for investment already, or they may not be; they could be property such as land and buildings. It's possible that the sale of one major asset can generate enough cash flow to see you through 30, 60, 90, 120 days.

Your opportunities here may include capital expenditures and large operating expenditures. Are there some projects you had planned that can be postponed? If there is a capital project or large operating expenditure that you can reasonably postpone, that's definitely an opportunity to improve your cash flow.

Potentially, another way for some major cost saving and the reduction in cash outflows is looking for opportunities to reduce your facilities footprint.

There are a couple of other points we wanted to mention when it comes to financing and investing. One is to be aware of the hidden risks associated with fair value accounting rules, which require companies to re-value certain assets and liabilities at market value every time they issue financial statements ("mark-to-market").

Think back to Lehman Brothers at the end of August of 2008. Lehman Brothers was going through a really challenging time in terms of getting people to buy their paper and in renewing the debt that they were rolling over, particularly at month-end and quarter-end. Because they had to pay premium prices for their financing instruments, and because they have mark-to-market accounting, Lehman Brothers had to write down the market value of those instruments. Essentially, what happened is, when Lehman Brothers was about to issue its August 31, 2008 financial statements, it had to significantly write down the value of these derivatives so much that the company was insolvent. The write-down — a paper entry, not cash flow — was more than the amount of capital on their books. That weekend, the Federal Reserve and the Treasury were put in the position of having to make an instant decision as to whether to bail out Lehman Brothers, like they'd done with Bear Sterns a few months earlier, or to let them publish their financial statements and let the market decide. As we know, they decided to let Lehman Brothers go bankrupt.

Why is this relevant to us today? It's an interesting example of how something as innocuous as a paper transaction, that is, a mark-to-market write-down of your financial instruments on your published financial statements, can have a dramatic, immediate real effect on your cash flow. It could have an immediate knock-on effect which could dry up your sources of financing.

Your Audit Committee should understand what the triggering events of default are in your loan covenant with your lenders. And if any of the things that we've talked about so far, such as trimming dividends, debt restructuring or asset sales, could result unintentionally in triggering an event of default, other events could also fall like a house of cards.

Make sure your lenders are onside with your financing strategy and the steps that you're taking to optimize cash flow. Lenders can really be your partner here. If you are the lender on the other side of the table, be sure to have that proactive, helpful conversation too.

Keep in mind that these steps are not your first or even second resort; that's why we call this theme "bridge the gap." These are last resort steps that you would take to keep the company's head above water. You don't want to do a distress sale if you can possibly avoid it. There are consequences to borrowing debt, raising capital or injecting your own money, too.

One of your financing strategies could be to buy or sell the whole organization. The ultimate last resort or distress is if your own organization isn't going to make it, and instead of a disorderly insolvency or a trustee, you could negotiate an acquisition or a merger of all of your operations with another organization.

We've focused almost exclusively in this chapter on companies that have been hit negatively by the pandemic, but what if you're one of the fortunate few whose business has benefitted from the current emergency? You may be in the position to buy other businesses who are failing.

There are plenty of opportunities out there. History shows us that the wealthiest people tend to do the best when everybody else is doing poorly. And people tend to make the most money through a recession because they have cash or buying power when prices of all kinds of commodities, including companies and shares, are depressed.

Whether you're in a not-for-profit or a for-profit, if you have opportunities to merge or acquire, to conclude some sort of business combination, why wouldn't you, as long as it's consistent with your mission, vision and long-term strategy? For example, in the not-for-profit sector, you could end up serving your clients better in the long run by putting together three or four organizations.

Theme 5: Refreshing the Budget

Our fifth and final theme is about the budget and the need for and timing of a complete refresh. How frequently should we be updating our financial projections or our operating budget? Rolling financial projections are reasonable in real time, but what is a realistic expectation to place on management in terms of submitting a complete operating and capital budget?

So, we pose this final question that a board will want to ask their CEO, the Audit Committee or the CFO:

At what point do we prepare a completely fresh operating and capital budget?

Let's recap what we've talked about so far. What we're dealing with in this chapter is financial direction, and it is the board's responsibility to set the direction of the organization at a financial level. Most of the time, we've been talking about the short run: 30, 60, 90 days. How do you make sure that financially you're able to survive the current crisis and come out of the other end of that with your head above water? We've used the Statement of Cash Flows as a roadmap for identifying opportunities to increase positive cash inflows, to reduce cash outflows and then to bridge the gap through financing and investing to have enough cash left at the end of the day.

But at some point, you're going to want to look at longer-term financial direction, which is the formal approval of an operating budget and capital budget for the next year.

What are going to be the drivers of deciding your long-term goals? These trace back to what we talked about in the first four chapters. To what extent you approve a change through your strategic plan cascades to changes in your performance and risk metrics, to changes in people and policy, and then finally your budget. They will cascade in that order; they'll drive one another, just like they normally would.

It starts with your strategy where we asked you, "To what extent do you expect your strategic goals and objectives to change as a result of the current emergency that we're going through?" Only 5% said none, 78% said some, 14% said most and 2% said all. So, the vast majority of people expect significant changes to their goals and objectives as a result of the current emergency.

That's the number one driver of updating your strategic plan in terms of when it needs to be done and the extent to which it needs to be done. And then, that will drive your business plan, which will end up with a fully fleshed out operating and capital budget.

Now, you're going to want to think about a couple of other things in terms of the timing of your new business plan and your operating and capital budget. What's your ability to confidently forecast what lies ahead? If you're still in shifting sands regarding a risk environment, it's probably too soon to expect a fresh operating and capital budget. Next, what's the capacity of management to handle multiple demands? Are they ready yet to be turning to an updated strategic and business plan including budget?

The short answer is, your CEO and your CFO hold the pen on the strategy, business plan and operating and capital budgets. This should be an ongoing conversation you have between your board and management. It will be driven by the extent to which your goals and objectives have changed, by your ability to confidently forecast and by your staff's capacity to realistically come back to you with a budget.

Key Questions for Refreshing the Financials and Projecting What Comes Next

Here is a series of questions boards can ask the CEO to gain reasonable assurance that your organization has refreshed the financials and has a good handle on what will come next:

Theme 1: Revenues

1. How confident are we that we have optimized opportunities to increase revenues?

Theme 2: Expenses

1. How confident are we that we have optimized opportunities to reduce expenses?

Theme 3: Cash Flow

1. How confident are we that we have enough cash for the next 30, 60, 90 days and beyond?

2. How confident are we that we have enough cash to weather the storm for the long haul?

3. How confident are we that we are optimizing your cash flow through working capital management?

Theme 4: Bridging the Gap

1. How might we bridge the gap?

2. To what extent do we need to consider a sale of your assets?

Theme 5: Refreshing the Budget

1. At what point do we prepare a completely fresh operating and capital budget?

CHAPTER 6
TAKING STOCK — MONITORING THE FINANCIAL IMPACTS

As we move into the second half of the book, we'll be turning our attention from setting strategic direction during and beyond COVID to the "control" side of governance: gaining reasonable assurance that the organization is going in the right direction during and beyond COVID. This monitoring and evaluation role of the board begins with asking the CEO these overarching questions in each of the five governance dimensions — and therefore each of the next five chapters (you will see these themes recur throughout the second half of the book):

How confident are we that we're "on the right track" through and beyond the current emergency?

How are we monitoring our success at weathering the current emergency?

How will we evaluate options for our path forward out of the emergency?

In this chapter we're going to focus on taking stock, including what questions and tools the board should be using to monitor and evaluate financial impacts on the organization.

Here are the six themes we will cover:

Theme 1: Liquidity

Theme 2: Profitability

Theme 3: Markets

Theme 4: Efficiency

Theme 5: Capital

Theme 6: Reassuring Stakeholders

Theme 1: Liquidity

Our first theme is liquidity. Not running out of cash is both the most important and most urgent imperative that you face. In an emergency, this is of particular concern.

Here are questions for the board to ask related to that immediate concern:

What ratios do we use to monitor liquidity, and what targets and tolerances have we set for these?

How have these been impacted by the current emergency?

How confident are we that we have sufficient liquidity to weather the emergency?

First, let's look at how organizations monitor liquidity.

The classic ratio for liquidity is called "working capital." This is when you compare current assets (assets that are going to mature and roll through cash in the next 12 months) to current liabilities (liabilities that will roll through cash in the next 12 months.) Working capital is simply current assets minus current liabilities.

Then there's a couple of ratios that take this one more step. One is to divide your current assets by your current liabilities: your "current ratio." This shows you what coverage or cushion you have. For every dollar of liabilities coming due, how many dollars of assets do you have to pay or cover them? A further refinement is a "quick ratio," where you only count assets that can be quickly turned into cash. This gives you a more realistic sense of cushion or coverage.

While each of these ratios is more refined than the former, they still miss major elements that can impact your cash. In some industries, like credit unions for example, these ratios may not be of any applicability at all.

A better ratio is a "debt-service ratio." This is your free cash flow divided by your committed principal and interest payment. This shows you how many times you can service your debt from your current cash flow.

If you have other commitments of cash that you know about, you should be adjusting your free cash flow (or its proxy, "EBITDA" — earnings before interest, taxes, depreciation and amortization) to take those commitments into account. You will want to understand what significant commitments or agreements you have. You will want to know what the chances of those being terminated or cancelled are due to the current emergency and how those cancellations might affect your cash flow.

There are a couple of other ways that you can measure cash in a not-for-profit. The "number of days' cash" that you have in a cash reserve fund is a popular ratio. Common targets of number of days' operating expenses that you have in cash is 60, 90 or 120 days. This has been life-saving recently, because a lot of charities and not-for-profits have seen their donations and their fundraising dry up through the pandemic.

Another tool you can use with liquidity is the number of days of receivables and payables. You can monitor those and influence your net cash flow by changing their pace. This can help you gain greater confidence in the adequacy of your liquidity. You can do the same with inventory if you're in the manufacturing or distributing or retail business.

Those are some of the main tools you can use to monitor and evaluate to answer the question, "Do we have enough cash?"

Theme 2: Profitability

A second set of financial ratios measures your profitability: "Are we making enough money?" Profitability ratios monitor your capacity to generate earning and therefore cash flow from operations in the first place. Key questions for your board to ask your CEO and CFO here are the same as when evaluating liquidity:

What ratios do we use to monitor profitability, and what targets and tolerances have we set for these?

How have these been impacted by the current emergency?

How confident are we that we have levels of earnings to weather the emergency?

Just like liquidity ratios, profitability ratios are going to vary industry to industry.

The most popular profitability ratios are "return on equity" or "return on investment" (ROI). These are particularly powerful when you compare them to your cost of capital.

ROI is when you take your net income or your earnings and divide it by your invested capital or your equity. Cost of capital is where you take your dividends plus interest that you pay and divide it by your debt and equity. So big picture, as long as your ROI is more than your cost of capital, you should be generating operating profits. You should be sustainable and profitable.

Another common profitability ratio is "gross margin." In some businesses, banks and credit unions, for example, it's the key ratio, the financial margin.

Gross profit is your total revenue minus direct expenses; gross margin is gross profit divided by total revenue to give you a percentage: how many cents on the dollar are being contributed by your net direct revenues and are available to pay your overhead and operating costs?

Particularly now in this emergency, you use this to calculate your break-even level of revenue; how much do you need to earn to pay all the bills, to keep the lights on? Divide your operating expenses by your gross margin. Take into account the effect of government emergency programs to calculate your minimum level of revenues that you're going to need to generate in order to be profitable. If you project to run below break-even, this gives management the opportunity to trim your operating expenses and overhead costs.

Beyond the enterprise as a whole, look at returns, gross margin and operating expenses by product line and by market segment. For example, what's your break-even level for your online sales versus in person? What's our ROI for the online market versus in-store sales? These give you a better idea of where you're driving profit and how you can drive more profits.

Theme 3: Markets

Our third theme has to do with markets. It's a good time to take a step back and think about what indicators we should be tracking as we map our way out of the emergency.

These are the key questions here for the board to ask the CEO:

How have our markets and clients been impacted by the emergency?

How have our competitors been impacted by the emergency?

How confident are we that we are optimally positioned in the marketplace coming out of the emergency?

Consider to what extent your markets and clients have been impacted by the emergency. Are you in a particular industry where the markets have been really hard hit, like the travel industry, airlines, tourism or hospitality? How have your clients been impacted? What about your competitors? Have they all been hit equally, or are some doing better than others, and why is that?

Benchmark yourself against well-performing comparators. Think about the retail sector — food and restaurants, for example. Many have taken a huge hit to their sales, but some have pivoted to takeout, delivery and online orders to drive top line revenues. Maybe you can drive sales through changes to your product-market mix through innovation.

Then, it's time to look at how confident you are that you are optimally positioned in the marketplace coming out of the emergency. Are you ready? Have you done what you need to do to shift for the longer-term market? What does that market look like? How likely is to return to its former self, or has it permanently changed? What will your industry look like in six months, in 12 months, in 18 months? How disruptive have these changes been, and how innovative do you need to be to succeed long-term? For every loser in a marketplace, there's a winner.

Your management is conducting ongoing environmental scans, particularly during the pandemic, and they are keeping their fingers on the pulse of your marketplace and on competitive intelligence. And so they should be able to report to you on a frequent and real-time basis.

For example, you're maybe in a better position now than before. A lot of clients are looking for a more reliable supply chain that's closer to home, in the same country as you're located. So, you may well be able to find a new group of clientele that you didn't have before because they're prepared to deal with you in order to have a sustainable and shorter supply chain.

International travel is going to affect all kinds of businesses like universities. How might you capitalize on that? You could take advantage of the fact that people aren't going to be travelling as far or might be doing distance learning.

There are all kinds of opportunities that you can take advantage of here because your marketplace has been disrupted. The board's role is to ask those questions and to make sure your management is thinking about and constantly scanning the marketplace. For example, in Canada, both Business Development Canada and Export Development Canada are excellent sources of market intelligence, including by types of industry and geographic region right across the country. Other countries have similar resources to macro-economic research for your industry and region. Your management can use these to benchmark your own financial impact and then to evaluate your different business models and alternatives going forward.

Theme 4: Efficiency

If you're a not-for-profit, then profitability ratios probably aren't as relevant to you. You will use efficiency ratios to track your productivity and efficiency instead.

The same questions we ask regarding liquidity and profitability also apply to efficiency:

What ratios do we use to monitor productivity, and what targets and tolerances have we set for these?

How have these been impacted by the current emergency?

How confident are we that we are efficient enough to weather the emergency?

Even more than liquidity and profitability ratios, efficiency ratios are industry specific, so it's much more difficult for us to identify exactly which ones will work the best for you.

Essentially, what you're looking at in efficiency ratios is line items of your operating expenses and comparing them to some kind of a benchmark in order to ask yourself how you are doing compared with those that are best practice in your industry.

For example, in a charity, you would compare your general and administration (G&A) expenses with every dollar in donations. Determine how much are you spending on G&A costs vs. donations. Then, benchmark that to other charities that are best practice in your industry, not just the average, because that's what you want to strive to be.

As another example, in healthcare, we look at full-time equivalent staff costs per patient. For every patient, how much are you dedicating in terms of full-time equivalent staff compared to other hospitals or clinics? The same efficiency ratio is used in education for students vs. staff.

In many cases, we begin with staffing expenses because it's often the number one expense in a service business and in many not-for-profit businesses, but you'll then want to look at other areas too. For example, examine IT expenses, facilities costs, marketing — anywhere you have a significant expense that you've got some discretion over and an ability to benchmark that with best practices elsewhere. Those are the kinds of things you're looking for in terms of efficiency.

You will also want to monitor efficiency in light of changes that have happened based on the COVID-19 emergency. For instance, you could be looking at a time where you're spending much more on IT because everything is virtual. It's a good reminder to be careful when looking at efficiency ratings and all financial ratios, too, because everything has to be understood in the context of the organization and the things you're doing and the reality that you face. Before you just cut an expense, look at the reality on the ground; maybe you need it more today than when you could meet in person, when you had staff in the office, when people weren't working from home.

Theme 5: Capital

Our fifth theme is capital.

Here are the questions the board can be asking the CEO in this area:

What ratios do we use to monitor capital, and what targets and tolerances have we set for these?

How have these been impacted by the current emergency?

How confident are we that we have adequate capital to weather the emergency?

The COVID-19 emergency impacts our financial health to the extent that we need to monitor our debt and make sure that our creditors don't force us into bankruptcy and shut us down. This means maintaining a sufficient level of capital.

Classic capital ratios are "debt to equity" and "capital adequacy." They essentially measure the same thing — the sufficiency of your capital cushion — but different industries use one vs. the other. Debt to equity measures your total liabilities compared to your owner's equity, share capital and retained earnings combined. It's sometimes called your "leverage" since it measures how much you've been able to "leverage" your owners' contributions through borrowings to grow your assets. Capital adequacy is total (equity) capital divided by total assets, so it expresses your capital cushion as a percentage: a leverage of 19 to 1 is the same as a 5% capital ratio.

Capital ratios are often in loan covenants with your primary lender and therefore are critical to stay onside with in order to avoid an event of default with your bank or credit union. If your projections show that the pandemic is risking your capital being off-side, then you may have to consider contributing more equity from the owners.

Particularly in small and medium-sized businesses, this is an area that you're going to want to weigh really carefully. You may be under a fair amount of pressure from your lenders to inject fresh capital, whether it's through shareholder loans or through equity itself, but you'll want to weigh the risks with new capital. That's why we put this theme fifth on the list. Before you put new capital into your business, you want to be comfortable that you've answered the questions around liquidity and profitability, and around your market and around your efficiency; you'll want to make sure you've got a good business model that is sustainable going forward. Otherwise, you may be "throwing good money after bad."

Another thing you'll want to think about is your own personal liability, both in putting new capital in or *not* putting new capital in. If you're getting close to the insolvency line, with the potential of your creditors petitioning you into bankruptcy and shutting you down against your control, as directors and officers, you're going to want to take a look at your alternatives and the effect on your own liability. In an insolvency, you may have unpaid wages, vacation, pensions and other deductions that you could be held personally liable for. But to avoid an insolvency, you may have to risk your personal life savings. This is a real-life test of what it means to be a fiduciary.

This leads us right into our final theme for this chapter. And that is, no matter what levels of debt you have, the key is to be proactive in communicating with your creditors and other stakeholders and in sharing with them your financial strategy and plan.

Theme 6: Reassuring Stakeholders

This final theme is really about reassuring stakeholders, creditors being key among them.

Here are a couple of questions for your board to ask your CEO:

How well have we engaged key stakeholders during the emergency?

How confident are we in the continued support of our creditors?

Broadly, you're seeking to understand in terms of crisis communications and crisis management how well your organization has engaged key stakeholders during the emergency.

Let's start over on the right-hand side of your balance sheet with your shareholders, who provide equity capital. Your shareholders legitimately need to understand what they can expect from your company performance and therefore their dividends. A lot of companies have suspended dividend payments or reduced them. A lot of companies have also suspended releasing earnings guidance, which is where you tell the market what you think you're going to post in terms of future financial results in coming quarters. While all of those things make sense, the more you do that, the more you create some unease, ambiguity and uncertainty in the minds of your shareholders. So clear, continuous engagement with investors will retain their trust and their continued engagement with the organization.

Once they understand what your plan is and that you have a plan that's plausible and reasonable and worth their backing, then further up the balance sheet as you go from equity to debt, your creditors need to understand how their debt is going to be serviced.

Creditors will appreciate you reaching out to them. Having spent much of our careers on the other side of that table in the lending business, we can assure you that your lenders would appreciate hearing from the people that have borrowed money from them. If you (your management) come in and sit down and walk through your plan, your fears and your opportunities with them, creditors in this time will be more than willing to be flexible in renegotiating terms of payment as long as you approach them in good faith with a workable plan.

Of course, you have some other stakeholders to think about. Your employees, suppliers, communities and other stakeholders seek confidence in your sustainability and in your capacity to continue operations and weather the financial impacts of COVID-19. Those are all groups that you're going to want to reach out to and reassure in a proactive way.

A couple of final thoughts.

One is internal controls. These may need to change with employees working from home, especially regrading cyber security and data protection. This has to do with making sure, at an Audit Committee level, your finance staff and your internal control staff are proactive in putting in place and testing internal controls as you shift what the workplace looks like and feels like. Those should be tested by your internal auditors and your external auditors on a regular basis.

And then finally, how has your financial disclosure calendar been affected by the emergency? Are additional continuous disclosures called for? Are extension and external filings required? How are you going to rewrite the risk section of your management discussion and analysis (MD&A)? Having that discussion around the board and Audit Committee table with staff ahead of time is going to help prepare everyone in advance to make sure you are disclosing how you're dealing with emerging and changing risk.

Key Questions for Taking Stock — Monitoring the Financial Impacts

Overarching Questions

1. How confident are we that we're "on the right track" through and beyond the current emergency?

2. How are we monitoring our success at weathering the current emergency?

3. How will we evaluate options for our path forward out of the emergency?

Theme 1: Liquidity

1. What ratios do we use to monitor liquidity, and what targets and tolerances have we set for these?

2. How have these been impacted by the current emergency?

3. How confident are we that we have sufficient liquidity to weather the emergency?

Theme 2: Profitability

1. What ratios do we use to monitor profitability, and what targets and tolerances have we set for these?

2. How have these been impacted by the current emergency?

3. How confident are we that we have levels of earnings to weather the emergency?

Theme 3: Markets

1. How have our markets and clients been impacted by the emergency?

2. How have our competitors been impacted by the emergency?

3. How confident are we that we are optimally positioned in the marketplace coming out of the emergency?

Theme 4: Efficiency

1. What ratios do we use to monitor productivity, and what targets and tolerances have we set for these?

2. How have these been impacted by the current emergency?

3. How confident are we that we are efficient enough to weather the emergency?

Theme 5: Capital

1. What ratios do we use to monitor capital, and what targets and tolerances have we set for these?

2. How have these been impacted by the current emergency?

3. How confident are we that we have adequate capital to weather the emergency?

Theme 6: Reassuring Stakeholders

1. How well have we engaged key stakeholders during the emergency?

2. How confident are we in the continued support of our creditors?

CHAPTER 7

COMPLIANCE — HOW WELL DID WE DO AND WHAT WOULD WE DO DIFFERENTLY IN THE FUTURE?

In this chapter, we discuss the policy side of monitoring and evaluation. When we deal with policy, first, we should be clear on what we mean by "policy." Policies at the board governance level are where the board and management team agree on the boundary line — the red line — between the board and management. It is under this line that management is going to operate the organization between board meetings. When over the line, they need to come back to the board for approval. Generally, that is what we mean by governance-level policy. We are answering the questions, "What are the parameters?", "What are the guidelines?" and "What are the lanes or landmines in the road?" Most organizations have a dozen or so board-level policies and so we suggest you proceed by first examining these over-arching questions:

How confident are we that we're "on the right track" through and beyond the current emergency?

How are we monitoring our success at weathering the current emergency?

How will we evaluate options for our path forward out of the emergency?

Here are the five policy-related themes we plan to unpack in this chapter:

Theme 1: Business Continuity Plan Effectiveness

Theme 2: Learning from our Mistakes

Theme 3: Learning from Success

Theme 4: Crisis Communication

Theme 5: Policy Refresh

Theme 1: Business Continuity Plan Effectiveness

Our first theme is the business continuity plan. Here are the three questions that we propose your board consider as you assess the effectiveness of your business continuity plan:

How well did we meet expected outcomes for continuation of operations?

How well did we meet expectations for service given the circumstances?

How might we improve (or create) our business continuity plan based on lessons learned?

A recent study found that two-thirds of UK organizations surveyed had no pandemic plans in place on the onset of COVID-19. A similar US survey indicated that 40% of boards did not have pandemic risk mitigation plans in place prior to the crisis. What most of us realize today is that when faced with a global pandemic, business continuity plans are critically important.

Many organizations had to wing it! They had to react and create plans in real time. Here's the problem. Reacting and winging it during a full-on crisis creates significantly greater risk. Without a playbook, the odds of making grave mistakes, missing things or heading down the wrong path are exponentially multiplied.

In the COVID era, business continuity plans have proven to be quite helpful as they provided guidance, stability, a roadmap and confidence in choices. Clearly these plans cannot anticipate everything, but at the very least, they cover the basics and provide a great foundation to build on.

This is what happens in a crisis: some organizations thrive, and others just don't survive. Some thrived because they were in the right industry to thrive. Others thrived because they had good plans, reacted quickly and were able to move quickly to make the needed shifts. A crisis is the time to act fast to avoid failing fast. If you're going to fail, you want to fail small and keep moving forward. Business continuity plans help to shift quickly towards what you can do now based on today's situation to drive revenue and growth, to move the company forward.

Some people have said that the COVID-19 pandemic was unforeseeable. The fact is, a pandemic is completely foreseeable. We know they're going to happen. We may not know when, but we do know from history that pandemics are foreseeable events. We also know that they are a major risk. These are scenarios that we should be able to put a business continuity plan together for. Long before COVID-19 hit North America, we knew something was going on in China. It was not a complete Black Swan. Though not something that happens frequently, pandemics do happen and are a foreseeable major risk that we can plan for.

Having a continuity plan in place is on the directional side of governance. So, let's talk about the control side. How did you do, and how could you do things better in the future?

Once the crisis is behind us, it is time to look at what went well and therefore what you should continue to do. What didn't go well, and you should stop doing it? Or what should you do completely differently? Where did your plans come up short? This gives you needed insight for updating them for the future, for the next time, and the next time and the time after that!

At the board level, the big question is, did the plan work? Did you get effective reporting back based on the outcomes? What did you expect to happen, and how close did you come to that? The board wants to have confidence. When we talk about the control side of governance in this area, the board is looking to gain confidence that the operations are successful, management is following the direction given them and the organization is moving forward successfully.

It's always easier to measure compliance and task completion. In other words, it's always easier to say, "Yes, we got this done." But, for a board to truly be successful, you need to receive outcome measures and understand the degree of success and overall achievement.

The purpose of emergency planning and drills is not because you can successfully predict what the next emergency is going to be, but to have your team get used to working together under pressure, even if it's a simulated emergency.

They will gain some muscle memory and strengthen their teamwork. This naturally leads us into our second theme: learning from our mistakes.

Theme 2: Learning from our Mistakes

There is much to learn from our mistakes. To not do so is a lost opportunity. COVID-19 has brought us many lessons learned, in some cases from what we have done well, but perhaps more so from our mistakes. This emergency provides us all with a great test on the extent to which we have a learning culture and are capable of learning from our mistakes.

Here are some questions the board can consider:

How well have we created a clear record of what went well, what didn't, where we got lucky and what we can do differently next time?

How might we establish a learning culture so that we can avoid the blame game and learn from our past?

What is the biggest mistake we made, and what did we implement to avoid it in the future?

In a crisis, we will be doing things we aren't used to doing. We're going to be doing things faster. We're going to be trying new things. So, we're going to make more mistakes than we normally do. That's not necessarily a bad thing if we learn from them and use them to help us move forward.

In a recent survey, organizations that had a crisis response plan in place fared better post-crisis by a margin of nearly two to one than those that did not. And equally, those that kept their crisis plan up to date and implemented lessons learned along the way were four times more likely to come out on top.

This is compelling data in support of preparing and having a good plan, but it's also about learning.

The last significant global pandemic was in 1918. That was a long time ago. Not many are around who remember that one. There were many lessons learned that can help us today.

That pandemic came in three waves, with the second being the deadliest. There was a mutation in the virus in the second wave, causing it to be more lethal. It shut the world down from 1918 to 1920. It lasted a long time. There is much to learn there that could have and may have informed today's pandemic crisis plans.

Boards should ensure the organization doesn't simply react and move forward. Rather, take the time to conduct a post-mortem and reflect on what was done well, what wasn't and where you just got lucky!

What this comes down to is proactively and positively using every opportunity, including the COVID pandemic, to reinforce a learning culture.

The goal of a post-mortem is not to find and ascribe blame. That will reinforce a culture of fear instead of one that learns. The focus should be on material missteps and mistakes, not on every little process that went wrong. The board should be concerned with strategic or multi-layered errors. It is here that you're more likely to find root causes and where you will learn the most. This will mean putting your egos aside and being open to reflection and retrospection without needing to play the blame game.

Post-mortems are not just something that's periodic — they're not just an event. They are a continuous process. It's never too early to begin or to start implementing improvements. If there's one thing that your board could say was a benefit from this emergency, it could just be this one thing: a healthy learning culture was instilled in the organization. The role of the board is to make sure you have a healthy organizational culture. It is management's role, led by your CEO, to lead in organizational culture formation.

Theme 3: Learning from Success

Even harder than learning from mistakes can sometimes be learning from success. Here are some questions for the board to consider:

> *How might we reset our risk culture to better embrace innovation, not just during the crisis but all the time?*
>
> *How might we engrain a culture of urgency after the pandemic?*
>
> *What went right, and what have we learned from our success that we will implement in the future?*

There really is a difference between learning from mistakes and learning from successes. Each requires a somewhat different mindset. When we are successful, we typically just keep doing what we are doing. It is common for us to be told "we learn more from our mistakes than we do from our successes." There's a growing body of research indicating that is not true. We learn as much or more from our successes, and we learn how to be successful as an organization from success.

There is a saying, "There's nothing like a good crisis to focus the mind!" The pandemic has caused organizations' leaders and teams to be highly focused. We have talked with several CEOs who report that their teams have never been more focused. Their people have never pulled together as much as they have of late. There's a real sense of urgency in organizations, and they are more innovative out of necessity.

Boards are asking, "How do we keep this up? How do we instill this sense of urgency and innovation into our culture going forward post-pandemic?"

One of the reasons we often aren't very innovative is we don't have a culture that looks for or rewards innovation. We oftentimes have cultures in the organization that are more worried about making mistakes and following procedure than they are about innovative solutions. Don't take this too far! If you're an air traffic controller, follow the procedures; don't be innovative! But for organizations that weren't overly innovative pre-pandemic, this new muscle has been developed because of the crisis. It's for this reason your post-mortem should include a review of both your failures and successes.

A learning culture has to do with ensuring that the organization is handling mistakes and risks in a healthy way. We're not punishing people. We're not burying things under the rug. We're not postponing learning from mistakes. We're doing everything we can to shine light in the dark corners and promote learning about them so that we can be more effective as an organization. This culture of urgency that we're talking about is about tapping into the kind of entrepreneurial spirit that I think many of our companies have felt throughout the COVID crisis.

A caution here: organizations cannot and should not attempt to sustain an emergency or urgent culture forever. People can't run full steam all the time. You will burn your people out. But what we're talking about here in this second layer of organizational cultural change has to do with not losing the momentum of that entrepreneurial spirit of innovation. We are talking about innovating, trying new things, being open to product and service market change, and leveraging successes so they're not just temporary flashes, but they're rooted and sustainable long-term.

Theme 4: Crisis Communication

It's time now to talk about crisis communication plans. Here are the questions the board should consider:

How do we define the success of our crisis communications?

What measures are in place that would indicate we successfully communicated with our stakeholders?

What is our Net Promoter Score pre- and post-crisis?

George Bernard Shaw is quoted as saying, "The single biggest problem with communication is the illusion that it has taken place." We don't know if we've really communicated until we have elicited some response or action from the people we're engaged with. Has the message we have communicated been received, understood, acknowledged and acted upon?

What we are seeing is a lot of boards asking specific details about crisis communications, like, "What platforms are we using?" "Did we use Twitter? "Did we use Facebook?" Did we do this?" "Did we go out to all of our stakeholders.?" "Did we get this stakeholder or that stakeholder?"

Those are all fairly operational and tactical questions. They're reasonable questions. There are certainly areas you would have interest in, but to truly understand whether you're successful with your communications, whether it be your communications protocol strategy or your crisis communications, you have to understand and define what success means to begin with. And you have to then put a measure to that. This is a measure of what happens as a result of that communication. What action did you ask for? And did you get that action or changed outcome?

For example, when you communicated to your employees, to what extent did they have an understanding of your message? For instance, if you were communicating to them that they can come back to work but they will have to wear a mask and physically distance, are they wearing masks, and are they physically distancing? You then know your communication has worked if they're doing the things you have asked them to do. And you should look to the same sorts of measures or outcomes for every stakeholder group you're communicating to.

Let's explore how you might apply the Net Promoter Score. This is a potentially impactful measure for any organization that goes far beyond just whether your communications plan is working. It was based on compelling research from Harvard, where researchers were able to narrow down to a single question that had a direct link to long-term profitable growth based on customer satisfaction. That question is, "Would you recommend our product or service to someone else?" And this research has driven a lot of companies to say, "We only need to ask two or three questions of customers, and this is one of them." And that leads to your Net Promoter Score. The majority of CEOs in the top 500 firms in the US use this specific metric and would say that this is their most important non-financial metric to understand how well the organization or the businesses is doing: the Net Promoter Score.

The research goes a little deeper. If a customer is a nine or a ten, then they are a highly satisfied customer, and you're essentially guaranteed that they'll be a repeat customer. You should concentrate your efforts on those nines and tens to significantly grow and grow your business.

Your Net Promoter Score is a great way to measure outcomes, including crisis media communications. What we're seeing in this pandemic is our communications need to be crisp, clear and empathetic. We need to show that we care as organizations — that we care about our employees and our customers. The drive that we're seeing right now is that those communications be inclusive about ESG and done in a way that is going to drive customer satisfaction, particularly with repeat customers, and so customers that would recommend us to someone else.

Theme 5: Policy Refresh

We decided we would focus our main themes in this chapter on the issues that were the most relevant when we did our research in terms of policy compliance and evaluation. So, this is a bit of a checklist on some of the other areas you want to make sure you have taken a look at in a policy refresh. Here are questions the board can ask the CEO:

Are virtual meetings beneficial, or should we alter our policy and only allow them in emergencies?

Is our delegated authority level to the CEO appropriate post-crisis?

What got pushed back from our board and committee work plans, and when can we reasonably reschedule this work?

How well did our work from home policies work, and is it time to update them based on the new reality?

Is our Investment Policy due for an update now that the pandemic is over?

We had talked about these five policies specifically in the direction side of policy (in Chapter 5), so we wanted to make sure we came full circle on those. We talked there about setting them and changing them; now, we need to gain confidence in how well they are serving us and to what extent they ought to be changed to reflect the "beyond COVID" world.

For a change, some of these questions are directed at ourselves and not necessarily management. For instance, on virtual board meetings, the board would be asking itself that question. You had to move to virtual meetings; what was that like for you? What were the benefits and costs, the pros and cons?

For example, holding virtual meetings could have given you the opportunity to have members who are remote participate in meetings more easily. It's a possibility that there are other benefits to virtual meetings. How did you do? How well did they work for you? Did meeting virtually work well enough or possibly even better in some areas to allow them beyond just in emergencies? Is this something you should adopt permanently?

Let's consider your delegated authority level. We talked about that in the earlier chapter, that a crisis is not the time to pull back the delegated authority and start looking over the shoulder of the CEO all the time. Yes, you may have meetings more often for updates, but it's actually a time where boards tend to delegate more authority to the CEO. They've got a really big job to do, and boards need to let them make decisions and run the business in order to move quickly in this time of crisis.

But when the crisis is over, or as it nears an end, it's time to ask, "How did that work out for us?" You may learn that your delegated authority levels prior to the pandemic were far too restrictive and you could have opened them up, or you may learn that you need to draw them back. This is a question that the board, once again, asks itself and comes back with the determination.

And then, what got pushed back from your board and committee work plans? When should you reschedule this work? During the crisis may not be the time for some of those things that aren't urgent. But let's not forget about them. Take a look at your work and ask, "How do we reschedule these back in now that the crisis is over?"

Consider working from home. We anticipate there's going to be a lot more work from home in the future. How well did that work for you? How well did your policies work? What is the optimal mix of working from home vs. returning to the workplace going forward? What are management's staffing plans and why?

Finally, is your Investment Policy due for an update? One of the things we have witnessed is significant swings in stock prices, with an early collapse and then rebounds. Did you pull back; did you make some changes to your Investment Policy because of that? Is it time for a little more risk? Post-crisis, would it be time to look at that again and say, "Where do we need to reset this? What are our lessons learned from the crisis? Were we too aggressive in our Investment Policy?"

As we wrap up this chapter on board-level policies during and beyond COVID, we're reminded of Dominic D'Alessandro, the long time Chief Executive Officer of Manulife Financial. He said that in times of crisis, the board drops the board-management line down. The board acts like a pendulum, swaying towards the extreme as the line between board and management drops way, way down. The board gets involved in all kinds of details in terms of tactics and operations, and getting into the kitchen. D'Alessandro cautions that it is much easier for a board to move the line down than to return to its "normal" way of drawing the line, being a governing-type board.

The purpose of this chapter is to invite your board to explicitly evaluate the effectiveness of your pandemic policies, what you've learned from these and how they ought to be written as we move beyond COVID. The overarching theme that we would encourage you to take out of this chapter is, do you need to show some intentional leadership as you emerge from the emergency in redrawing that line at a sustainable level and making sure that you return to our level as a governance, strategic oversight board, not an intervening or an operating board? What's in the best interests of the organization and all your stakeholders?

Key Questions for Compliance — How Well Did We Do and What Would We Do Differently in the Future?

Overarching Questions

1. How confident are we that we're "on the right track" through and beyond the current emergency?

2. How are we monitoring our success at weathering the current emergency?

3. How will we evaluate options for our path forward out of the emergency?

Theme 1: Business Continuity Plan Effectiveness

1. How well did we meet expected outcomes for continuation of operations?

2. How well did we meet expectations for service given the circumstances?

3. How might we improve (or create) our business continuity plan based on lessons learned?

Theme 2: Learning from our Mistakes

1. How well have we created a clear record of what went well, what didn't, where we got lucky, and what we can do differently next time?

2. How might we establish a learning culture so that we can avoid the blame game and learn from our past?

3. What is the biggest mistake we made, and what did we implement to avoid it in the future?

Theme 3: Learning from Success

1. How might we reset our risk culture to better embrace innovation, not just during the crisis but all the time?

2. How might we engrain a culture of urgency after the pandemic?

3. What went right, and what have we learned from our success that we will implement in the future?

Theme 4: Crisis Communication

1. How do we define the success of our crisis communications?

2. What measures are in place that would indicate we successfully communicated with our stakeholders?

3. What is our Net Promoter Score pre- and post-crisis?

Theme 5: Policy Refresh

1. Are virtual meetings beneficial, or should we alter our policy and only allow them in emergencies?

2. Is our delegated authority level to the CEO appropriate post-crisis?

3. What got pushed back from our board and committee work plans, and when can we reasonably reschedule this work?

4. How well did our work from home policies work and is it time to update them based on the new reality?

5. Is our Investment Policy due for an update now that the pandemic is over?

CHAPTER 8
EVALUATING HOW WE DID — BOARD AND CEO EVALUATIONS POST-CRISIS

Boards are seeing CEO evaluations popping up on their annual work plans. They're having to decide if they're going to go ahead and do these evaluations or if they are going to defer them until COVID-19 is in the rear-view mirror. They have been asking, if they are going to go ahead now, what will that evaluation look like? How will it look different than in previous years? The following overarching questions provide the foundation for considering the finer points of board and CEO evaluations:

How confident are we that we're "on the right track" through and beyond the current emergency?

How are we monitoring our success at weathering the current emergency?

How will we evaluate options for our path forward out of the emergency?

This chapter is therefore devoted to the topic of board and CEO evaluations post-crisis following these six themes:

Theme 1: Why Evaluate?

Theme 2: When do We Evaluate?

Theme 3: How Should We Evaluate?

Theme 4: Which Criterial Should We Use?

Theme 5: What Should We Compensate?

Theme 6: What Board Evaluation Methodology Should We Use?

Theme 1: Why Evaluate?

If the board decides to go ahead with the CEO and board evaluations, they will want to first answer these questions:

Why are we evaluating our CEO?

What are the expected outcomes?

Why are we evaluating the board?

What are the expected outcomes?

As organizations navigate the COVID-19 pandemic, we have found that CEO and board evaluation practice is all over the map. There's no single consistent practice here. In many organizations, the CEO is typically scheduled for the end of the first quarter. Because there are so many December year ends, the end of the first quarter is the end of March. That was the beginning — the early days of the emergency. Evaluations of the CEO and board quite rightly were deferred. Now, months later, there is a bit of a burning platform in many organizations where your CEO evaluation is in many cases overdue, and it may well be coinciding with a board evaluation at the same time.

The best place to begin would be to think about the "why" question. At the end of the day, you're going to have to use your own business judgment in discussion between board members and the CEO about which parts of your CEO and board evaluation to proceed with sooner rather than later. Your answer's going to be driven by "why." Why are we conducting a CEO evaluation and board evaluation now?

There are several different reasons or outcomes you will hope to achieve. One common reason for conducting evaluations is learning. Formal evaluation gives you an opportunity once a year to lift your heads from the busyness of board business, to take stock of how you're doing and to learn what you could be doing better. This reason alone is quite valid today, even during an emergency.

This is a great opportunity for the CEO and the board to check in with each other, to take a pulse check and to make course corrections. Many of you are going through significant strategic shifts. The CEO and board evaluations need to check in with one another in terms of how you are doing, what you are doing well, what you could be doing better; these check-ins could be highly valuable. How you do those evaluations could be quite different than how you would conduct evaluations for other purposes.

Another reason to conduct evaluations is for accountability. This is when you conduct evaluations as a formal mechanism to draw a line under the year and check on how well you've each performed. This reason may or may not be valid at the height of a crisis. Your question then is going to be, is there utility in deferring it further until things are more settled? And if so, when, when would you do it? Most boards deferred the accountability evaluation to the fall. The main implication to deferring the formal annual accountability mechanism until then is related to CEO compensation as boards typically use the results of the annual CEO performance evaluation to approve incentives and merit compensation for the year.

Here again, you want to exercise your business judgment as to whether this is the right time for these evaluations. Some organizations are deferring them. Having said that, you may have a contractual obligation under an employment agreement to go ahead with compensation arrangements with your CEO. You may have a moral obligation when your CEO is probably working harder and under more pressure than ever before. So even though these things are popping up on your board work plan, and you've perhaps deferred them one meeting cycle, maybe two or even three, you'll want to ask the question and discuss with your CEO.

Everything in evaluation flows out of the "why." Yet, so often, boards will jump right to the "how" without even thinking about asking the "why." But the "why" drives the "how." It drives what you ask. It drives what you're evaluating against. It drives the alignment between the efforts of the CEO and their compensation.

Theme 2: When Should We Evaluate?

Once your board and CEO have agreed on why you're moving forward with an evaluation, assuming that you've chosen to evaluate the CEO and potentially the board, too, the "when" question prompts itself next. We have three questions for you to consider when it comes to when:

When should we conduct the CEO's evaluation?

Are there elements of the CEO's performance management that should be deferred?

When should we conduct the board evaluation?

If you've decided that you should go ahead with a more formal pulse check at this point, then you're ready to move on to the "how." But if you've decided to continue to hold off on a formal accountability evaluation, at the very least, you should plan for and decide on when. Will you push it an entire year and just take a pulse check now with one another?

Our advice is don't just punt, punt, punt, under the assumption that the current emergency is going to quickly end and things will suddenly return to normal. That's like not a fair assumption. So, if you are going to defer the CEO accountability evaluation and compensation, have a plan as to when you're going to defer it to. Do the same thing with a board evaluation as there's probably not as much urgency to doing a formal evaluation of the board.

Many boards have chosen to go ahead with a board evaluation as they find this a healthy time to be looking at how the board's functioning and how the chair is functioning in terms of learning and communication. Again, if you're going to defer, agree and discuss your rationale and when you're going to defer to. Then you're ready to move on to the "how."

Theme 3: How Should We Evaluate?

Once you're clear on the purpose and the timing, you can move on to "how." You may want to vary your methodology. There are lots of ways to evaluate. We typically use six different tools for board evaluation. Some of them are much more complex than others. You can conduct a valuable pulse check that doesn't take a lot of the board's time but brings good value to the board.

Here are some questions you will want to ask:

How will we evaluate the CEO?

Will we use a questionnaire and/or interviews and/or other tools?

How will we evaluate the board?

Will we use a questionnaire and/or interviews and/or other tools?

Many boards don't want to do full-on survey questionnaires right now for their CEO and board evaluations. Instead, they are looking to conduct a short, pulse-check questionnaire that is comprised of a handful of questions — maybe 10, 12 — that speak to getting your finger on the pulse of the progress. What can you learn, big picture, about how the CEO and the board are doing right now and have done since the beginning of the pandemic? Then, they tend to supplement that with one-on-one interviews with each of the board members, the CEO, and in many cases, with members of the senior management team.

This approach will help you answer the "why" question in terms of learning and communication feedback, but not necessarily the accountability compensation question. Now, if you've decided to go ahead with the accountability and compensation side of your CEO's evaluation, then you probably need to conduct a more extensive questionnaire to benchmark the CEO's performance to agreed targets and results, and to approve incentive and merit compensation based on that.

What you don't want is for your evaluation to be an exercise in compliance — a checkbox evaluation. Many times, boards decide they will just use the same process or questionnaire that they've used in the past. Avoid checkbox approaches by ensuring whatever process you use is designed to add value to the organization.

Theme 4: Which Criteria Should We Use?

That lead us to criteria. There is a myriad of choices that you face in terms of criteria and the measures of success that you're going to be thinking about. So, your next questions are around criteria:

Which criteria will we evaluate our CEO against?

Should we vary the weightings due to the emergency?

Which criteria will we evaluate the board against?

This is a tough one. Currently, we're seeing real tensions and sensitivities around answering this question. This is because on the one hand, the simple solution is simply to pick up where you left off. Just evaluate the CEO against the metrics you agreed to at the beginning of last year. But so much has changed, the vast majority of which is outside of the control of the CEO. The results for year-end will likely bear no resemblance to what your CEO projected at the beginning of the year. And so how do you reconcile that? How can you be expected to fairly evaluate the CEO against those metrics when so much has changed?

There is a second parallel challenge. That is, how might you recognize that your CEO may be working harder and maybe more effectively than they ever have before? They are keeping the organization going. They may be missing many of the pre-agreed targets but are highly successful in navigating the emergency and keeping the organization from becoming a statistic. We are seeing some interesting, innovative solutions, and these alternatives may help you think through how you're going to deal with this challenge.

One solution has been to change the criteria for the performance evaluation away from the measured targets, the metrics from year-end, more towards your level of confidence that the CEO is leading you in the right direction in each area. So, you would keep your scorecard, but instead of using your year-end targets, you would supplement, or in some cases, replace them with a measure of confidence that your CEO is leading you in the right direction and taking the right steps in each of those areas. By measuring confidence, what you're doing is taking into account that a lot of the current outcomes are probably outside the CEO's direct sphere of control, potentially even outside their sphere of influence. Is it fair to hold the CEO accountable for things that are outside their control or even outside their influence? The answer is not black and white. This is a question of judgment and dialogue, but by evaluating how confident the board is that the CEO led the organization during the emergency, that can help you with the learning and communication and process improvement.

Measuring your degree of confidence through asking the following pulse-check questions might be a fairer, more equitable and forward-looking way to conduct your CEO evaluation:

How confident are you that the CEO responded quickly and decisively?

- How well did they identify and deal with emerging risks?

- How well have they protected employee health and wellbeing?

- How well did they put in place a continuity plan?

Another alternative is to change the weightings of what is important. This too is not without controversy. Anytime you change something from what was agreed to at the beginning of the period, you run the risk of introducing subjectivity. The point is, during an emergency, the priorities of the organization will change. With COVID, employee health and wellbeing, risk management, business continuity and liquidity, among other factors, have increased in importance compared with some of the other areas of organizational scorecards. For some, these may need to change significantly. For others, less so.

You can apply the same principles to your board evaluation, too.

Some have not adjusted the scorecard weighting; rather they have focused more on the CEO's leadership in effective engagement of key stakeholders like investors and creditors. How they are handling the emergency and putting a clear roadmap in place to guide the organization through the emergency are probably much more important macro questions than the normal questions you would ask.

Therefore, interviews can be a more robust tool than just questionnaires in this type of evaluation. Interviews are well-suited to getting more complex and nuanced feedback from evaluators.

Changing criteria mid-course, or worse, after a CEO has accomplished what was asked of them, is problematic. How fair is it to ask a CEO to accomplish certain things in a year, which they do, only to change how you evaluate and compensate them? This is what many organizations are facing. They have contracts with their CEO and other executives. They have CEOs who have met their objectives and qualified for their incentive compensation and bonuses for the period just prior to COVID-19 hitting. There is often a lag between year-end and when the bonus is paid out. Potential financial hardship for the organization, or the optics of paying bonuses for the prior period when employees are being laid off in the current one, leaves boards in a tough position. So, timing is a big issue.

Theme 5: What Should We Compensate the CEO?

CEO compensation is frequently a sensitive discussion which provides an easy opportunity to go off the rails. With compensation, it's less about getting it right and more about not getting it wrong. At this particular moment in time, these three questions will help you make sure you're all on the same page so that there's no white space between you and the CEO.

How might we be fair in compensating our CEO at this time?

How might we ensure consistency with executive and employee compensation?

How might we communicate what compensation was earned, how and when?

How and when is perhaps the most important question of all, because getting compensation wrong is almost always about communicating compensation poorly. There are three directions you could go, and we've seen organizations take each one of these. Some argue, go ahead, follow the contract and pay the agreed-upon incentive pay for the prior period. The argument is that the board has the obligation to compensate the CEO for the at-risk pay that they've earned and that you shouldn't think of this as a bonus or even call it a bonus. That's a misnomer. You entered into a contractual agreement with your CEO stipulating that if the CEO hit these targets, they will not only earn the fixed portion of their pay, they'll also earn the at-risk portion of their pay regardless of what happened related to COVID-19 — good, bad or ugly. That's something that was earned. Some have managed to navigate through the emotion, focus on the facts and make a choice to move in that direction.

Others have chosen to pay the CEO an additional bonus at this point in recognition of the fact that they are going through such a difficult, challenging time. Some consider this a retention bonus that the CEO deserves, not because of a contractual agreement but because of the emergency.

The third path some have chosen is to defer all or part of the at-risk or incentive compensation for their CEO for the foreseeable future. This is primarily because of inconsistency with other executive and employee compensation. If you're laying people off or asking staff members to take cuts in hours or cuts in pay or job share, how can it be consistent with paying incentive or at-risk compensation to the CEO and potentially other senior executives, even if they've earned it during a better time?

This is a question about business judgment. It's a question of removing emotion. That doesn't mean removing perception. The board will want to consider how this will land on people.

CEOs too are handling compensation issues from one end of the spectrum to the other. Some are demanding the letter of their contract be honoured and their incentive compensation be paid to them. Some are at the other end of the spectrum and are refusing their incentive compensation. We have even seen CEOs of large not-for-profits accept their annual incentive compensation and/or bonus and then donate it back to the organization.

There is no single right answer. It's going to depend on your current situation and

There is no single right answer.

context. Our best advice is to shine light on it. Have your board and CEO get together, reach a meeting of the minds and then find a way to communicate whatever fair and consistent path you've chosen. Make sure that all the different parties affected by this are onside.

Theme 6: What Board Evaluation Methodology Should We Use?

Board evaluation should be less problematic than your CEO evaluation. This is because we generally evaluate the CEO based on organizational outcomes results, but we evaluate the board on its effectiveness in governance. This is largely unchanged by COVID-19. Here are some questions that we have for you to consider in this area:

How will we evaluate our board at this time?

Will we change our methodology and criteria?

How will we evaluate our chair at this time?

We have been touching on the board evaluation as we've been going through this chapter, but we wanted to make sure that we highlighted it specifically as a theme. You may choose to link the way in which you evaluate your board to the choices you've made around the CEO. There's some resonance to that. In other words, if you've chosen to go ahead with your CEO's performance evaluation or pulse check, it makes a lot of sense to do the same kind of thing with the board in parallel. If you've chosen to go with a short-form questionnaire but supplement that with interviews for the CEO, maybe you do exactly the same thing with the board: short-form, pulse-check questionnaire, supplemented with interviews.

As we said earlier, unlike the CEO, there's no need to evaluate the board on a series of measurable, quantifiable performance outcomes. But it's a good time to get feedback on how the board's doing. This is a critical emergency that we're going through. It's not over yet, but it's far enough along in that you can pause and do a useful pulse check. You will want to check that the board is providing effective oversight.

During this emergency, some boards have become quite interventional and operational. This might be an opportunity to hold up the mirror and catch that. Also, if you're doing your board evaluation in conjunction with a CEO evaluation, the results of the two can be synergized and combined.

If you're going ahead with an evaluation of your board, you also perform an evaluation of your chair. The chair plays an essential liaison role between the board and the CEO, a relationship that is under unprecedented pressure. You will want to know how well the chair is playing that role. Is the chair striking the right cadence in engaging with the CEO and in a meeting with the CEO? Do they have the right frequency, rhythm, degree, level and scope of interactions with the CEO so that the chair is being a resource, a sounding board and a feedback mechanism for the CEO without unempowering or micromanaging them?

There may be less urgency to go ahead with committee and committee chairs or individual director evaluations. It may be wise to defer these for a time. It's going to depend on the degree to which the current emergency still has some urgent activities and priorities that the board and its committees are facing.

In an emergency, a light touch, a high-value evaluation should be the order of the day.

Key Questions for Evaluating How We Did — Board and CEO Evaluation Post-Crisis

Overarching Questions

1. How confident are we that we're "on the right track" through and beyond the current emergency?

2. How are we monitoring our success at weathering the current emergency?

3. How will we evaluate options for our path forward out of the emergency?

Theme 1: Why Evaluate?

1. Why are we evaluating our CEO?

2. What are the expected outcomes?

3. Why are we evaluating the board?

4. What are the expected outcomes?

Theme 2: When do We Evaluate?

1. When should we conduct the CEO's evaluation?

2. Are there elements of the CEO's performance management that should be deferred?

3. When should we conduct the board evaluation?

Theme 3: How Should We Evaluate?

1. How will we evaluate the CEO?

2. Will we use a questionnaire and/or interviews and/or other tools?

3. How will we evaluate the Board?

4. Will we use a questionnaire and/or interviews and/or other tools?

Theme 4: Which Criteria Should We Use?

1. Which criteria will we evaluate our CEO against?

2. Should we vary the weightings due to the emergency?

3. Which criteria will we evaluate the board against?

Theme 5: What Should We Compensate the CEO?

1. How might we be fair in compensating our CEO at this time?

2. How might we ensure consistency with executive and employee compensation?

3. How might we communicate what compensation was earned, how and when?

Theme 6: What Board Evaluation Methodology Should We Use?

1. How will we evaluate our board at this time?

2. Will we change our methodology and criteria?

3. How will we evaluate our chair at this time?

CHAPTER 9

THE NEW CORPORATE PERFORMANCE SCORECARD — SETTING A NEW STANDARD

Risk and opportunity are really two sides of the same coin. They go hand in hand. You don't have one without the other. This chapter builds on and weaves together some of the learnings from the earlier chapters. Previously, we identified some promising metrics: financial and people dimensions. Now we're going to bring those together, along with some others, into a single corporate performance scorecard — a conceptual framework that takes a step-by-step approach to building an integrated corporate performance scorecard. Here are the overarching questions for this chapter:

How confident are we that we're on the right track through and beyond the current emergency?

How are we monitoring our success at weathering the current emergency?

How will we evaluate options for our path forward out of the emergency?

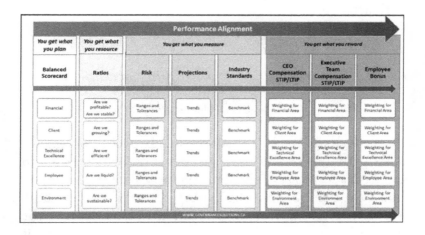

In this chapter we will look at the performance scorecard through the lens of five themes:

Theme 1: Scorecard Dimensions — The Changing Expectations

Theme 2: Ratios — The Financial Metrics of your Scorecard

Theme 3: Risk — Ranges and Tolerances that the Board will Use

Theme 4: Projections — Trends and Benchmarks

Theme 5: Alignment — System and Compensation Alignment

Theme 1: Scorecard Dimensions — The Changing Expectations

We begin with the scorecard dimensions and the changing expectations around those. This is where you get what you plan! The questions your board's going to want to begin with are as follows:

What changing expectations will impact the scorecard?

What does "success" look like going forward?

What core dimensions or goal areas should frame the scorecard?

Let's firstly be clear about the line between governance and operations in this area. One, it's not the board's job to create this scorecard. This is management's job. Management holds the pen on this. They will propose what they think are the right ratios, risks, projections, etc. Two, it is the board's job to ensure the scorecards are in place. If yours is a small organization with a volunteer board and almost no staff, this may differ. The board will have input into the scorecard and make sure it gets created. Three, it is the role of the board to approve the scorecard. Four, the board will use the scorecard to monitor the performance of the CEO and the organization going forward.

> You don't just get what you plan. You get what you plan, what you resource, what you measure and what you reward.

We have a saying in governance: "You don't just get what you plan. You get what you plan, what you resource, what you measure and what you reward." That means you must be sure to build a scorecard that covers all four of those areas: planning, resourcing, measuring and rewarding. That covers the breadth of a scorecard.

You will also want to cover the depth of a scorecard — the different dimensions and goal areas of a balanced scorecard.

The Balanced Scorecard model[4] is one that classifies any organization into four dimensions generally called goal areas. This tool is intentionally designed to capture and simplify your business model, whether you're for-profit or not-for-profit, large or small. The four dimensions are learning or innovation (often called people or employees), process (or quality), customers (also called client or stakeholders) and financial.

People engage in high quality operational processes to produce excellent products and services. Those products and services are then delivered to your clients or customers. Clients and customers are delighted by them and love to use them. Customers continue to buy the products and services, and sales revenue is generated. That's the way we think about Balanced Scorecard — as a simplification of our business model in the for-profit world. In the not-for-profit world, we use the same scorecard dimensions, but we reorder them with the financial dimension at the bottom.

We raise financial resources and then use those resources to equip and motivate people: employees and volunteers. Those people engage in operational processes to produce high quality products and services. And those delight our clients, customers, beneficiaries, students, patients — whatever they're called in our sector. And that is really our ultimate mission. The client dimension is the pinnacle of the balanced scorecard in the not-for-profit world.

At Governance Solutions, we have added a fifth dimension to create what we call a "balanced scorecard plus." The fifth dimension is called environment. This dimension

---

4   The Balanced Scorecard model was first introduced by Robert S. Kaplan and David P. Norton

represents ESG: environment, social, and governance and involves the aspects of the business model, such as social responsibility, environmental stewardship and governance, that are felt to be missing from the traditional four dimensions of the scorecard. This is a way of saying you should customize your dimensions to your business model, to your organization.

You likely already have a scorecard in place at your organization. As we go through and beyond an emergency, it might change and need a proactive approach to transformation.

Every scorecard begins with your strategic and business plan. Your scorecard is a tool that summarizes the key measures of success for your organization overall. Therefore, to build an effective scorecard, you first must have a clear picture of what success looks like for your organization and understand how that's changed because of the emergency.

We know that goals and objectives are going to change. Our research show that only 5% of companies believe that they will experience no changes to their goals and objectives coming out of the pandemic. The other 95% believe their organization will change from some to a great extent! Those changing expectations will cause you to shift your scorecard. For some, these changes will be minimum — minor tweaks and adjustments. For others, the change will be dramatic. For all, you get a really good opportunity to measure the resiliency of your company and of your strategic plan.

There are parts of your scorecard that are not going to change: efficiency, productivity and profitability. These key financial metrics are there to stay, and you want to keep them in your scorecard. But when you go through tough times, you want to be able to measure the capacity of an organization to absorb shocks.

An example is to intentionally introduce diversification as a strategy to contribute to an added objective of resiliency.

An organization could measure and report in their corporate scorecard geographic diversification by geography, product line, business line, market segment diversification, product lifecycle, industry, etc.

Another change you might want to see is heightened priority of workforce health and safety as a measure in your corporate scorecard.

Theme 2: Ratios — The Financial Metrics of your Scorecard

Our second theme is around ratios: the financial metrics of your scorecard. This builds on that recent discussion we had with you about ratios in Chapter 6. The three questions you will want to consider around your boardroom tables are these:

What financial ratios should be in the scorecard?

What are other measures of our financial success?

How will these be impacted by the emergency?

Any emerging risks and opportunities from the current emergency should now be reflected in your selection of financial metrics for your corporate performance scorecard. These may not be the same last year versus next year.

Though we may be in the midst of a deep recession with no clear pathway or timeline to recover, we have optimism that there'll be a recovery. The ongoing tightness in the economy and in jobs that affects spending in many of our sectors is affecting our revenue stream. So, we're seeing a single-minded focus on liquidity — on making sure we have enough cash to survive. Organizations that didn't really worry too much about liquidity before are looking at one or two key liquidity ratios and metrics on a constant basis to make sure that management is generating efficient net cash to survive. There is also an aversion to debt despite cheap and easy money.

Interest rates are low, and we've got high liquidity. We could also expect government policy, regulatory policy and even tax policy to become less friendly as the months go by as governments seek to claw back some of the funds expended during the height of the emergency. Securing a reliable supply chain, probably closer to home, is high on management agendas, and so scorecard metrics related to reliability are key. A great example of that recently is in all the frontline medical supplies, including PPE and items like that.

Revenue generation from online sales and diversification strategies are other metrics boards are looking at closely: the extent to which they've been able to offset the revenue drops and other more traditional areas from new areas of revenue. This deals with the question around emerging risks and changing expectations and how we might expect financial metrics and ratios to change.

And then we have the classic ratios we talked about in Chapter 6 that are designed to answer the questions, "Are we profitable?", "Are we stable?", "Are we efficient?" and "Are we liquid?" And we briefly mentioned what we call horizontal and vertical ratio analysis, which is a tool to help us answer the two additional questions: "Are we growing at the right level?" and "Are we sustainable?"

Boards will want to agree on key financial ratios and metrics from these different families and that are influenced by the emerging trends and shifts in your marketplace — those that best measure success in your organization from a financial perspective in the financial dimension.

You'll notice that the way we've created the scorecard (seen above), you can use financial ratios, too, as proxies for how you're doing in other areas, for example, in the people or client dimensions, not just in the financial dimension. This provides you with a truly robust and high-level enterprise scorecard. It has enough indicators that you're not overwhelming the board with 30, 40 or 50 different financial ratios. Yet, it is broad enough that you're testing the strength of your income statement, balance sheet, profitability and efficiency, and your liquidity and stability.

Mid-cycle changes may need to be made to your scorecard in an emergency. For example, you might need to make some changes to your business plan, policies, the delegation of authority or your budget and therefore to how you're going to measure, monitor and evaluate success. You might need to make some modifications in the short run simply because continuing to use the old measures is no longer relevant.

Having said that, making alterations is different than doing a complete refresh. Some of you may need to do a complete refresh and create a new corporate performance scorecard. Doing this in the middle of an emergency may not be optimal. You will want to wait until you've caught your breath and you have enough clarity about your strategic plan going forward; that's when you're going to refresh the whole scorecard.

If your complete strategy is changed, your scorecard is not meaningful. A refresh will be needed to align with the new strategy. But if you've only got a couple of tweaks on your strategy, then your scorecard at mid-emergency with just a few tweaks might still be just fine. Typically, you would refresh your scorecard annually. When you update your strategic objectives in your plan and you update your risks, normally the updates to your scorecard would be informed by that dialogue.

Theme 3: Risk — Ranges and Tolerances that the Board will Use

We are at the "you get what you measure" aspect in the scorecard matrix, where we set risk ranges and tolerances. Your board's going to want to think about these questions:

What key metrics and targets should we select for each non-financial scorecard dimension?

How might we agree on ranges or tolerances for each known risk area?

How might we describe ranges or tolerances for each unknown risk area?

For many organizations, a silver lining of the onslaught of COVID-19 was the ruthless prioritization of strategic objectives. That means there are fewer metrics and objectives that boards and management teams are much more focused on. Boards want assurance that management is not losing sight of running the business, so they have been ruthless and targeted on the most significant and meaningful strategic objectives.

There are parts of our corporate performance scorecard that don't change. These are the core strategic objectives that the organization needs to achieve, whether in good times or bad. There's just a small number of core metrics that don't and won't change. They stay the same and help the organization stay the course. This applies the principle of materiality to the scorecard. We are asking of every single one of these measures, "Do they really matter?", "Are they substantive?", "Are they material?" and "Do they really make a difference to the organization living or dying, succeeding or failing?" If they are not material, remove them from the scorecard. Remember, just because you've taken something out of your board-level scorecard, that doesn't mean it's not being measured. It just means it's going to be cascaded down to a sub-scorecard within the organization in a business unit. It doesn't need to be at the board level.

Make sure that between board and management you've agreed on a small number of strategic objectives and that they are SMART[5].

The primary deliverable of a strategic planning system is to have a small number of agreed-upon SMART objectives. Once you've got those, management will come back to you with proposed targets and ranges for each objective. The target is the number you would expect to hit if your assumptions in the budget are right. The range has to do with the tolerance that you have as an organization for missing that target. What's the minimum and the maximum level that you would still be okay with?

In Chapter 3, we introduced you to the concept of known and unknown risks. We return to that concept briefly here because the way in which we set tolerances, that is to say the range of acceptable outcomes around the target for an objective, differs depending on whether it's a known or an unknown risk. For known risks, it's reasonable for us to set numerical tolerances. Liquidity is an example. Perhaps we have a target of 180 days cash as a reserve. Because of the nature of the risk, we could have an important dialogue about our tolerances. We can set a lower threshold — let's say no less than 90 days. And we can set a high-end threshold too because there's a cost to holding too much cash. There should be a reasonable cap on holding cash for future reserves — let's say 270 days.

---

[5]   SMART objectives are specific, measurable, attainable, resourced and time-bound.

That's a fairly wide tolerance. So, our target for that measure is 180 days, but we would tolerate anything between 90 and 270 days. Narrower ranges reflect lower tolerances.

Unknown risks don't lend themselves to measurable tolerances. It is, therefore, more difficult for us to set numerical target ranges. In some cases, the best we can do is to agree on a narrative — a written description of our tolerance for each of these objectives.

Sometimes boards throw items into the unknown risk category when they don't really belong there —for example, reputation risk or leadership succession risk. It might seem like those are qualitative, but having said that, we may be able to come up with numerical proxies for both. For example, people count the number of negative and positive mentions of your company in the media as a proxy for reputation risk. You can set a tolerance of no more than two senior vacant management positions at any one time as a proxy for leadership succession risk. These are good examples of how, when you persevere and engage in a deeper dialogue between the board and management, you can come up with some really good proxies and flesh out the breadth of your scorecard.

Theme 4: Projections — Trends and Benchmarks

Our fourth theme is setting projections and using trends and benchmarks, which is still part of the "you get what you measure" columns of the scorecard matrix. Here are the questions your board will want to ask and answer:

How will we set reasonable growth rates for our scorecard metrics?

What metrics must stay the same?

How do external standards and industry benchmarks inform
these metrics?

Bob Biehl, author, and executive mentor to several Fortune 500 corporations, is of tremendous help here. He teaches that there's two kinds of metrics in a scorecard:

1. What must go up and up and up?

2. What must stay the same?

These are those metrics that measure of the health of your organization. Those that must go up and up he calls vital signs. An example might be revenue growth. Those that must stay the same he calls critical standards. An example here might be number of days of cash. Once you've hit a high enough standard, you don't need to keep improving. You just have to keep hitting that mark.

This is a very useful way of thinking about setting projections. By differentiating between "what must go up and up and up" and "what must stay the same," you can focus your board-level performance scorecard on metrics that matter and reflect the health of your organization.

We should mention here that you'll want to be aware of any external commitments or covenants that your organization has made, particularly to your lender, for example. We are not encouraging the board to micromanage. But, if there is an external agreement in a collective bargaining agreement or a loan covenant, or a regulation from government that management's aware of, you will want to find a way to put a red circle around it or indicate that on the scorecard. There are some external consequences if you miss this target.

You will not want to forget the importance of industry comparisons or benchmarks. You have chosen the dimensions that form the framework for your scorecard. And, you have chosen the financial ratios and metrics to measure financial performance. You have even chosen some non-financial metrics and set some targets, ranges and tolerances. You've looked at projections and growth rates and "what must go up and up" and "what should stay the same." You have one more step before you are done.

It's time to benchmark those against best practices in your industry. What organizations are doing best in each of the dimension areas? How are they doing? Because unless you've taken that step, you don't really know as a board, or as a CEO, that you can have confidence that your targets are robust. This step takes a lot of work. Even though it's not easy, it is the best way to validate and have confidence in your metrics, targets, ranges and tolerances.

We hear all that time from CEO's and boards that "We can't really use those benchmarks. We're too unique. Everybody's different from us or we're different from everybody else." There's some truth in that. Every person, every company, is unique. But there's always a benchmark. It may not be a particular company in all areas. Maybe you're going to have to use three or four different companies and pick a benchmark on a particular metric from each of these. And you may have to adapt some of the benchmarks. For example, in the healthcare industry, there's lots of benchmarks, but you may have to adapt for size and scope.

It takes work. Even though every organization is unique, that's not a reason not to try setting benchmarks. Without benchmarks, you don't know how far under the bar you're operating. Maybe you'll find your way over it. And that would be an exciting thing to celebrate!

Theme 5: Alignment — System and Compensation Alignment

This brings us to our fifth and final theme for this chapter: aligning compensation and performance reward design with your corporate performance scorecard. This is the "you get what you reward" columns of our scorecard matrix. Your questions here are below:

How might we best align our CEO's compensation with the new scorecard?

How might we be confident that the CEO is aligning executive and employee compensation?

How might we be confident that our entire performance management system is aligned?

In a previous chapter, we dealt with people evaluation and making the tough decision about compensating our CEO and executives based on past performance during a crisis. In this chapter, we are switching gears and asking ourselves how we might set new targets for the coming year.

In a perfect world, the CEO's, executive's and employee's compensation and performance reward design should align with the main elements that lead to the corporate performance scorecard. For the CEO, you should expect something like a 75 to 80% correlation between the performance targets in the CEO's evaluation and the corporate performance scorecard. As you go further down the organization, the alignment will drop off because the CEO is accountable for achieving the whole performance scorecard, executives are responsible for slices of it, and so on. The board sets the CEO's compensation. All of which to say, the better informed the corporate performance scorecard is, the better informed your CEO's compensation system is going to be.

Both the overall design of your CEO's compensation and the annual incentive awards will be driven by the priorities and measures of success that you've developed in your corporate performance scorecard. In fact, the whole point of this matrix, this conceptual framework, is alignment. The board's job is to make sure that management has created a performance management system beginning at high-level balanced scorecard dimensions and ending in compensation that is aligned both vertically and horizontally.

All the pieces should fit together and inform one another. That might sound like common sense, but the larger your organization is, the more difficult that is. The larger the organization, the more complex it is and the more advisors it may have. There may be a strategic planning advisor, risk advisor, governance advisor, financial advisor, performance management advisor and so on. These multiple advisors may never meet with one another, never talk to one another and report separately to different vice presidents or executives who are building the pieces that your CEO and board want to make sure are integrated.

Ensuring alignment will involve a back-and-forth iterative conversation to make the pieces align and integrate smoothly. This brings us back to the first question in Theme 1 of this chapter: "What changing expectations will impact the scorecard?" To the extent that you've agreed which dimensions and selected objectives are going to be higher priority in the future than they have been in the past due to the current emergency, you'll need to adjust the weightings to reflect them. The board should expect the CEO would apply the same rationale to executive and employee compensation.

Just to be clear, the board only sets the CEO's compensation. The board does not do this in a vacuum. This is a conversation that takes place between the board (usually through the HR and Compensation Committee) and the CEO.

Building your scorecard is a journey, not a destination. It is an ever-changing work in progress at the best of times, but more so in an emergency like COVID-19.

If yours is a smaller organization, start by measuring only three or four things. This will help the board focus on governance rather than operations. And even if the board members are volunteers, it will focus at least part of your board meeting on governance, setting strategy and monitoring results. And that's a healthy thing.

A final piece of advice when building board-level scorecards: keep it simple! One of the rules of thumb we use in scorecards is that every time you add a measure, you should take another measure out. You are going to be weeding that garden. This idea is to continually prioritize and decide about usefulness. Management goes to a lot of work to track and report against metrics, so make sure they matter. You will be asking, "Is this metric useful to us?", "Do we ever use it?" and "Would it matter to the board if we didn't get this measure?" You'll be able to tell as the years go by which measures are more valid and helpful and which ones really aren't. Maybe they're better as exception indicators that management monitors and tracks but then only reports to the board on them if they're out of kilter.

Key Questions for The New Corporate Performance Scorecard — Setting a New Standard

Overarching Questions

1. How confident are we that we're on the right track through and beyond the current emergency?

2. How are we monitoring our success at weathering the current emergency?

3. How will we evaluate options for our path forward out of the emergency?

Theme 1: Scorecard Dimensions — The Changing Expectations

1. What changing expectations will impact the scorecard?

2. What does "success" look like going forward?

3. What core dimensions or goal areas should frame the scorecard?

Theme 2: Ratios — Financial Metrics of your Scorecard

1. What financial ratios should be in the scorecard?

2. What are other measures of our financial success?

3. How will these be impacted by the emergency?

Theme 3: Risk — Ranges and Tolerances that the Board will Use

1. What key metrics and targets should we select for each non-financial scorecard dimension?

2. How might we agree on ranges or tolerances for each known risk area?

3. How might we describe ranges or tolerances for each unknown risk area?

Theme 4: Projections — Trends and Benchmarks

1. How will we set reasonable growth rates for our scorecard metrics?

2. What metrics must stay the same?

3. How do external standards and industry benchmarks inform these metrics?

Theme 5: Alignment — System and Compensation Alignment

1. How might we best align our CEO's compensation with the new scorecard?

2. How might we be confident that the CEO is aligning executive and employee compensation?

3. How might we be confident that our entire performance management system is aligned?

CHAPTER 10

REINFORCING CONFIDENCE WITH YOUR STAKEHOLDERS — KEEP THE CONVERSATION GOING

Having come all the way around the governance circle, in this final chapter, we are going to focus on reinforcing confidence with your stakeholders, on keeping the conversation going. Once again, we will leave you with a series of relevant questions that, together with those in the nine other chapters, collectively build your governance roadmap "through COVID and beyond."

Just to remind you, this is a roadmap and not a calendar with the timing attached to each of these steps. Each of the steps discussed in this book calls for a discussion among your board, CEO and management team in terms of when you might implement them. For some of you, it could be right away, for others, it could be several weeks down the road and for others still, it may be several months into the future.

Together, the second half of this book is focused on "control," and so all five of these chapters are collectively intended to help us answer these three overarching questions:

How confident are we that we're on the right track through and beyond the current emergency?

How well are we monitoring our success at weathering the current emergency?

How will we evaluate options for our path forward out of the emergency?

This chapter focuses on the strategic control level of the governance framework. At this level, we are dealing with macro issues of accountability. Who are the board and the organization accountable to? This leads to questions around disclosure, transparency, reporting, stakeholder engagement and social responsibility. This includes the broader accountability of the board and the organization, not only to your internal stakeholders and your owners, but broadly to your external stakeholders beyond the owners.

These are the themes we will be exploring in this final chapter:

Theme 1: Reinforcing Stakeholder Trust

Theme 2: Integrating ESG

Theme 3: Evaluating Environment

Theme 4: Ensuring Social Capital

Theme 5: Monitoring and Enhancing Human Resources

Theme 6: Monitoring the Business Model and Innovation

Theme 7: Evaluating Governance

Theme 1: Reinforcing Stakeholder Trust

Your board should not assume that trust with stakeholders has been eroded during the emergency, nor should the board just assume that all is well. You may well have had no challenge with your stakeholder trust levels during the current emergency, and these could be in really good shape. It may be just a question of making sure that you sustain and maintain your performance in that area.

But a lot of things have happened quickly, and a lot of trust has been shaken. Here are the questions that we would propose the board ought to be seeking answers to overall around stakeholder trust:

How confident are we that we have the trust of our stakeholders?

How are we measuring our success at gaining trust with our stakeholders?

How will we evaluate options for enhancing the trust of our stakeholders?

If we look at just one piece of research, the Adelman survey, they look at trust across sectors. Historically, CEOs have ranked quite a bit higher than government officials or health authorities in being trustworthy. However, in their most recent survey conducted in May 2020, 60% of respondents said CEOs need to take the lead in addressing the pandemic, while only 28% felt CEOs were doing a good job of that.

That survey ranked CEOs last amongst their group of peers, including government officials and health authorities. This shows us that the emergency has turned trust on its head. The research is showing us that there is a desire for organizations to be more than just profit centres. The expectation is that organizations have a responsibility to consider all stakeholders when they make decisions. This is consistent with the Supreme Court of Canada's ruling in the Bell Canada Enterprises (BCE) case that directors owe a fiduciary duty to all stakeholders, that no single stakeholder group has primacy, including the shareholders.

On a global level, CEOs are coming forward, saying, "We have a responsibility beyond our shareholders to be good citizens and to be looking to be sustainable, not just driven by short-termism and profits." BlackRock's CEO and the Business Roundtable have widely publicized manifestos that call for stakeholder value creation as opposed to just shareholder value creation. The pandemic is accelerating and amplifying this call from the public. A crisis or a pandemic can erode trust in institutions and erode trust in businesses, raising levels of skepticism.

What can we take away from this research, from this shift in people's perceptions? Stakeholder value-based decision-making, and flawless, proactive communications are more vital than ever. You really need to look at all your stakeholder groups — consumers, lenders, suppliers, employees and owners — to do all you can to build trust with them.

The crisis may have really hindered your ability to do business. This crisis has put different stressors on different organizations in different sectors. Some sectors may have stressors across all those stakeholder groups; others, for instance, may see online sales booming and have stressors in other places — in fulfillment, for example. Some industries that ship a lot of goods are experiencing significant problems getting things delivered as they move far more product than they have ever done. They experience stressors with their customers because they are struggling to meet demand levels they did not anticipate. Others are dealing with stressors with their owners, shareholders and lenders.

Boards need to understand what groups are most affected and how. This calls for ensuring effective, proactive communications with each group to understand them and assure them, "You've got this." You, as the board, understand what their problems are. You have plans that you can recover or you can effectively expand as needed if that is the case.

To be confident that your decisions and communications are reinforcing the trust of your stakeholders, you will want to monitor these closely and develop measures of success for each stakeholder group.

In an earlier chapter, we talked about Net Promoter Scores as a highly effective measure of trust for customers. Along with that, you will need to receive measures of success for other groups as well, for example, your suppliers. A potential way to gauge whether suppliers still trust you would be to monitor your credit terms with them. As a matter of form or good governance, this is not the type of measure that boards are going to look at normally, or often; that needs to be one of your Key Performance Indicators (KPIs), but it might be one of those measures that make it to your scoreboard as an exception indicator. If that number falls below a certain level, or if there is a big movement in how much credit your suppliers are willing to give you, then the board needs to know. You should consider a lot of these measures for some stakeholder groups in that vein. The board does not need to see a thousand measures, but it does want to understand big swings or changes that may indicate a stakeholder group has lost trust in the organization.

Employee engagement for employees, and to a lesser extent employee turnover, are the measures you are probably already used to and may already have on your scorecard. You may want to monitor shareholder activism, share price or member satisfaction if you are in a not-for-profit or a cooperative. You will want to monitor your credit facilities and rating classifications. Once again, this could be an exception report. For example, if the bank makes significant changes to your credit availability, then the board needs to know that.

Depending on how the pandemic affects you, each of these stakeholder groups should be monitored. Some will be more important to you than others. Your management should establish measures of trust for each key stakeholder group. Together, you should agree on whether this is a scorecard measure or an exception indicator. You will want to agree on target ranges: what is acceptable, and what will trigger action?

Keep in mind, you are testing and validating the degree of confidence you have as a board that your trust level with your stakeholders is in good shape.

Theme 2: Integrating ESG

Here are the three questions that we would propose the board seek answers for in terms of integrating ESG into your roadmap:

How confident are we that we have a fully integrated and financially material ESG program?

How robust is our ESG reporting and disclosures?

How will we evaluate options for enhancing the materiality of our ESG program?

Nowadays, most investors recognize that ESG and maximizing profits are not mutually exclusive. Integrating ESG is not like the old days of corporate social responsibility (CSR), when we made disclosures on how much corporate giving we did and how many volunteer hours our employees served, and that was the end of it. Integrating

ESG is meant to tie together the social benefit and the sustainability of the organization and then integrate that with our strategy and reporting.

ESG initiatives should provide material financial benefit to the organization. It is not "either-or;" it is "both-and." Your ESG plans, initiatives and programs should benefit society and your bottom line, and they should be prioritized in that way. This means integrating your strategy, enterprise risk management, and environmental, social and governance programs.

Some of the most material aspects of ESG related to the pandemic are risks around employee and customer safety and opportunities around practices like working from home, which could impede, or which can lead to employee satisfaction and environmental benefits. By looking at both sides, you can see that the pandemic and your response to it has created both risks and opportunities within the ESG area. You will dig more deeply into specific areas as you review ESG by area. However, big picture, boards need to be making sure that ESG is aligned with strategy and targeted material risks and opportunities.

Integrated disclosure and reporting on ESG is one way to do that and one place that the board has visibility to the organization's ESG. This reminds us of the famous quote by the Supreme Court Justice Brandeis, that "sunlight is the best disinfectant."[6]

How do you make sure that the people inside your organization from the very top to the very bottom are behaving in a way that is in alignment with the expectations of society and the expectations of the communities in which we walk and work and breathe? Sunlight is the best way; the

---

6   Louis D. Brandeis, *Other People's Money: And How the Bankers Use It*, (New York: Frederick A. Stokes Company, 1914), 92.

more transparent you are in your disclosure, the better the board can ensure accountability of the organization. And that is how a board ensures that light is shone in the dark corners of the organization, right through the organization in ESG practices.

The challenge in ESG disclosure is that, unlike financial accounting, there is no single framework that is generally accepted around the world. In the world of financial accounting, there is a set of rules that we follow — guidelines and accounting principles. And if we follow those, we can prepare our annual report or financial report to be consistent with those. That is not the case with ESG; sadly, there is no single framework. The good news is, there are two or three frameworks which are broadly in use. The most popular by far is called the Global Reporting Initiative (GRI). GRI has been adopted by over 700 of the 1200 largest companies around the world. Number two is the United Nations Sustainability Development Goals. And number three is the Carbon Disclosure Project, which is more about, as you would expect, greenhouse gas emissions. Organizations tend to adopt that framework if they are in a sector where the primary disclosure is around reducing emissions. These are not mutually exclusive; you can adopt all three if you want it to.

Therefore, one of the discussions you want to have between your board and your management team is guided by this question: "What integrated ESG reporting and disclosure framework are we going to follow?" And then a follow-up question has to do with the external validation of your ESG reporting. Just like you have an external auditor for your financial reports, how are you going to make sure that there is some external testing and validation or attestation of your integrated ESG results?

Theme 3: Evaluating Environment

At this point, we are going to discuss ESG alphabetically, starting with environment. The three questions that we would propose your board be thinking about under the theme of the environment are these:

How confident are we that we have implemented environmentally friendly programs?

How are we monitoring the success of our environmental programs?

How will we evaluate options at the board level coming from management for enhancing our environmental footprint?

Concern for the environment was one of the top news stories globally before the pandemic hit us, and there is still healthy interest.

Companies are taking it seriously; organizations are taking it seriously. While it would be an ideal world if we all took every element of ESG equally seriously, from a trust and corporate reputation perspective, we tend to focus on those things that are most material to us. So, if you are in heavy industry or extraction, you will be focused on carbon emissions as that is where stakeholder trust can be built or eroded. Or if you are at UPS or Purolator and delivering product, the idea of implementing optimized routes with electric or hybrid vehicles that can reduce your current footprint and have a bottom-line result is obvious "low hanging fruit" in the environment area of ESG.

You may be able to do good for the environment while helping your financials — a "win-win." But that is not always the case; there are all kinds of changes that we could make to help the environment, but not all of them will necessarily benefit the bottom line.

Bringing it back to COVID-19, interestingly we have seen that the physical environment is healthier and the air is cleaner all around the world because people are not travelling as much. This impact stems from both airplanes not flying and people working from home rather than commuting. We have seen pictures taken from satellites of some of the most polluted cities and rivers in the world showing how just these few months of significantly reduced economic activity is having a major positive impact on the environment. According to one study, even working from home half-time, for those that could in the US, would save 51 million metric tons of carbon going into the atmosphere. Essentially, all the cars running in New York for a year would be saved.

You can look at it this way: the pandemic allowed us to do a trial run on people working from home to figure out whether we could make it work. And one of the benefits of that, if we can make it work, is it is going to be better for the environment. Wouldn't it be great if we could restore economic value creation without losing a bunch of that environmental progress?

We have been involved at Governance Solutions in ESG reporting and in carbon emission reporting for most of the 29 years that we have been in business. In fact, we were early engaged in the Carbon Disclosure Project, for example. And one of our observations is, it is much easier to adopt carbon emission reporting today than it was even five or ten years ago. The science behind it and the way in which you can estimate your emissions of carbon both directly and indirectly, even in the service business, are accessible to all. We would encourage you to see if there is a way in which your organization can join that and add your voice to measuring ESG by carbon emissions. And by doing that, you set targets for reducing your carbon footprint, which of course, is the whole point of adopting and implementing these global codes.

This is a good reminder to be wary of your ESG strategy becoming solely a marketing strategy rather than a values-based strategy. That is what they call "green washing" — pretending to embrace ESG and environmental sustainability to boost the company's brand rather than aligning legitimate ESG programs with overall corporate strategy and priorities, including your values. What you want to do is start with your values, value creation and stakeholder value creation.

Theme 4: Ensuring Social Capital

Now it is time to switch gears to the second part of ESG: "social," and the next theme we call social capital. Here are the questions that we would propose the board ask in the area of social capital:

How confident are we that we are living up to our social license, our license to operate?

How are we monitoring the success of our contribution to society?

How will we evaluate options for enhancing our social capital?

The social part of ESG is broken down into a number of different parts: our contribution to society, which allows us to have a social license but also encompasses human resources; the management of relationships; human rights and the protection of vulnerable groups.

One of the things that has impacted us layered on top of the effect of the COVID-19 pandemic is the horrible death of George Floyd in Minneapolis and the worldwide condemnation of systemic racism, led by the Black Lives

Matter movement. That has basically changed the conversation around race and equity and justice, not just in United States and Canada but around the world as well.

Interestingly, Reddit co-founder Alexis Ohanian found the movement so compelling that he announced he was going to resign from their board and that he wished for his seat to be filled with an African American candidate. It is a request that the board has indicated it is going to honour, because what we are talking about is not just words but deeds, not just the talk, but how we are going to walk the talk at every level of society, including at the board level.

Different organizations are going to have different responses. Some will tweet support, some will give funds and donations to causes and charities. Some will examine their policies around hiring and promotion. Some may do nothing or stay quiet, but each of these choices has consequences and has an impact on your corporate reputation and your social capital.

So, your board, whether you like it or not, has a role to play in championing, and meeting in conjunction with your CEO, your response to these calls for justice and equity when it comes to human rights and to society broadly.

You will want to carefully consider your engagement and the fact that words without deeds will not be enough. In other words, you will want to avoid greenwashing. This is well past the stage of just issuing press releases; this is about taking concrete action.

Your board will want to understand your corporation's strategy around human rights, the protection of vulnerable groups and transparency around the demographic makeup of staffing and promotions within the organization.

Other aspects of social capital that you will need to incorporate into the questions that you ask management are about the quality of your products, affordability and customer privacy. There is no doubt that the pandemic has put strain on the availability of some of our products and services.

Theme 5: Monitoring and Enhancing Human Resources

In the area of human resources, the board should be thinking about the following:

How confident are we that our HR and employee safety programs are effective?

How are we monitoring the success of our HR programs?

How will we evaluate options for enhancing our HR programs?

You will see that we have intentionally unpacked human resources from the social envelope. That is partially because HR has been affected so much by the pandemic.

Our workforce and workplaces have been impacted by the pandemic to the extent that the board has some serious big picture questions to ask about employee health and safety, work activities and labour relations. How well has the organization ingrained a safety culture within the organization?

"The Economic Times" of India says 71% of companies in a global survey list employee safety and wellbeing as their top business priority right now because of the COVID-19 pandemic.7 Companies everywhere are being judged, both

---

7   Sreeradha Basu, "Employee safety top priority of companies, finds survey of COVID-19 impact," The Economic Times, last updated June 3, 2020, https://economictimes.indiatimes.com/news/company/corporate-trends/employee-safety-top-priority-of-companies-finds-survey-on-covid-19-impact/articleshow/76177320.cms.

in the court of public opinion and potentially in the legal courts of the land, on how well they treat employees during this time, especially around keeping them safe.

You could quickly and noticeably fail in this area if you do not take proactive steps. When we think about employee safety in terms of a heat map, for instance, both the impact and the likelihood of employee downtime have increased significantly in most organizations due to the COVID-19 pandemic.

One of the things we have encouraged you to do with ESG is to integrate it with your enterprise risk management, and when it comes to employee health and safety, that should be mapped with your ERM risk map. You should have expected it to have moved up and into the right on your risk map. Boards should treat employee safety as a material risk in all industries.

Even if you have historically had minimal risk in this area, and at the risk of repeating ourselves since we have talked about this in the people and the scorecard chapters already, you should definitely make sure that your roadmap through and beyond COVID-19 deals with this area of workforce health and safety. The big takeaway for boards is thinking about your roadmap in terms of its enhanced risk profile.

Theme 6: Monitoring the Business Model and Innovation

The next topic is your business model and innovation. These are the three questions that we propose for you to ask in this area:

How confident are we that our value creation process is optimized?

How are we monitoring the success of our business model?

How will we evaluate options through enhancing our value creation processes?

What we are talking about here is how we create value. How well we have integrated innovation into value creation, and what methods do we use to drive value?

Many organizations have become — or have had to become — much more innovative as a response to the pandemic. They are taking a hard look at their business models in light of the "new normal" — everything from supply chain to product packaging for online sales and delivery.

Throughout this book, we have talked about strategy and how most organizations are looking at significant changes to strategy because of the pandemic and because of the changes associated with coming out of it. On the other side, we expect significant societal changes to occur, from working from home to having virtual meetings to online shopping. We could see significant changes with all our stakeholder groups, employees, suppliers, consumers and even lenders. Simply the ability to have virtual meetings versus in-person meetings could change how we conduct business going forward, changing the landscape of our business and the environment.

Does our business model fit the new normal?

Boards need to ask, "Does our business model still fit the new normal?" "Did we learn things during the pandemic that will allow us to improve our processes or improve our products or offerings?" "Can we do that in a way that will enhance our ability to drive value or to want to ensure that appropriate consideration is given to innovating and adapting?"

Theme 7: Evaluating Governance

Our final theme in this chapter is governance, the "G" of ESG. Here are the three questions that we would encourage you to ask in this final area of governance and leadership:

How confident are we that we are leaders in corporate governance?

How are we monitoring our success in governance leadership?

Do we have a diversity strategy with meaningful targets for the board and management?

The governance dimension of ESG encompasses a wide range of topics including regulatory compliance, risk management, safety management, conflicts of interest, anti-competitive behaviour, corruption, bribery, executive compensation, lobbying, political contributions and policies. In other words, good governance. In many ways, we have touched on this during each chapter of this roadmap.

For example, we talked earlier about executive compensation during the pandemic and how it has complicated variable compensation decisions. We are also seeing some boards delaying or deferring regular board and CEO evaluations because of the pandemic. Once people have a chance to catch their breath, these evaluations will need to resume to ensure healthy oversight and continuous improvement.

There is renewed pressure and consideration for enhanced diversity within organizations in leadership and on boards. At Governance Solutions, we have long been advocates for board diversity, not just because it is the right thing to do societally, but because the research clearly shows that it enhances and improves governance performance.

We have been privileged to be leaders of global thought on this subject for many years, being the co-authors of

"Women on Boards: Not Just the Right Thing...but the "bright"Thing,"[8] which is the most widely cited publication about diversity on boards around the world.

Interestingly, before we wrote our report on women on boards, we were told that organizations must wait to have women on boards until there is a sufficient number of women on management teams. However, our research told us that the opposite is true: until there is a critical mass of women on boards, you are not likely to see a critical mass of women on the management team. If we apply that to diversity in general, including ethnic and heritage representation in management, where the real power is, it has got to start at the board level.

Women on Boards... touches on gender as a proxy for true, broad diversity on the board. But race, i. e. ethnic heritage diversity, is another area that is hugely underrepresented on boards and in senior management. In many jurisdictions, public companies are required to disclose their diversity strategy and targets. Even if you are not a public company, this is still a governance best practice.

Therefore, you should have a diversity strategy for your board and for your management team that sets some meaningful targets and a roadmap that outlines a strategy towards how you are going to get there. Again, this is moving from words and greenwashing to walking the talk.

We end with a challenge for each of you to adopt a meaningful diversity strategy.

In this final chapter, we are weaving together the threads of all the chapters before it. When it comes to your business model, we spent a fair amount of time throughout this book

---

8   David A. H. Brown and Dr. Debra L. Brown. "Woman on Boards: Not Just the Right Thing...but the "bright Thing," Volume 341 Issue 2, Conference Board of Canada, 2002.

on questions the board should be asking management on your new business model, on innovation and diversification, and related opportunities and risks. We encourage you not to just take this chapter as a standalone but to weave together your roadmap from the earlier chapters into a single fabric.

Key Questions for Reinforcing Confidence with Your Stakeholders — Keep the Conversation Going

Overarching Questions

1. How confident are we that we're on the right track through and beyond the current emergency?

2. How well are we monitoring our success at weathering the current emergency?

3. How will we evaluate options for our path forward out of the emergency?

Theme 1: Reinforcing Stakeholder Trust

1. How confident are we that we have the trust of our stakeholders?

2. How are we measuring our success at gaining trust with our stakeholders?

3. How will we evaluate options for enhancing the trust of our stakeholders?

Theme 2: Integrating ESG

1. How confident are we that we have a fully integrated and financially material ESG program?

2. How robust is our ESG reporting and disclosures?

3. How will we evaluate options for enhancing the materiality of our ESG program?

Theme 3: Evaluating Environment

1. How confident are we that we have implemented environmentally friendly programs?

2. How are we monitoring the success of our environmental programs?

3. How will we evaluate options at the board level coming from management for enhancing our environmental footprint?

Theme 4: Ensuring Social Capital

1. How confident are we that we are living up to our social license, our license to operate?

2. How are we monitoring the success of our contribution to society?

3. How will we evaluate options for enhancing our social capital?

Theme 5: Monitoring and Enhancing Human Resources

1. How confident are we that our HR and employee safety programs are effective?

2. How are we monitoring the success of our HR programs?

3. How will we evaluate options for enhancing our HR programs?

Theme 6: Monitoring the Business Model and Innovation

1. How confident are we that our value creation process is optimized?

2. How are we monitoring the success of our business model?

3. How will we evaluate options for enhancing our value creation processes?

Theme 7: Evaluating Governance

1. How confident are we that we are leaders in corporate governance?

2. How are we monitoring our success in governance leadership?

3. Do we have a diversity strategy with meaningful targets for the board and management?

AFTERWORD

Governing in Scary Times is based on a series of online learning events developed and delivered in the spring of 2020, during the immediate throes of the COVID-19 pandemic.

At the time of publishing, the second wave is well underway with vaccine distribution taking place. Hope is on the horizon, and a sense of relief is building. An end appears to be in sight.

And yet, the effects of the crisis will continue for some time.

The good news is that we have all learned some things through these scary times. The principles and messages discussed in this book reflect that learning and they remain relevant for us. The questions posed in each chapter provide a roadmap for your board to follow — one that will help you remain resilient and focused on your role, work through the effects of the pandemic with foresight, and stay the course.

Boards can apply these principles and messages as you work through those continued effects, and for that matter, refer to them in any emergency or crisis you may face in the future.

Our desire is that you find this work of value to your organization and board — a helpful roadmap that guides you step-by-step through and beyond these scary times.

ABOUT THE AUTHORS

Dr. Debra L. Brown, David A. H. Brown and Rob DeRooy together have 75 years of direct and practical experience working with boards. Comfortable and confident with both boards and executives, they possess a mix of well-researched, experiential and conceptual insights that uniquely qualify them to advise organizations on governance. All have served as CEOs, reporting to boards and been board members of varied organizations, including as Board and Governance Committee Chairs. They can see governance issues from both sides of the boardroom table. They know what works and even more importantly, what does not!

ABOUT GOVERNANCE SOLUTIONS

As globally respected leaders in all things governance, we work with organizations and directors to unlock the full potential of their boards through our integrated portfolio of products and services. Our superior solutions offer everything you need to optimize your board.

www.governancesolutions.ca

OTHER BOOKS BY THE AUTHORS

Today's board members need more tools not more rules!

Governance Solutions: The Ultimate Guide to Competence and Confidence in the Boardroom is chock full of governance tools that make the complex seem simple and bring order to the chaos. This is not just a book "about governance", it tells you how to "do governance".

Authors David A. H. Brown and Dr. Debra L. Brown deliver:

- Proven Governance Solutions: It is a single source—the ultimate guide—for solving your governance problems.
- Access: It includes almost 70 governance concepts and tools that are unique only to this book.
- Competence and Confidence: It covers the broad spectrum of governance issues from governance structure and process, through boardroom leadership, culture and behaviour.
- Answers! It tells you not only what works, but as importantly what does not work in governance.

With so many spotlights trained on corporate boards, there could hardly be a better moment for hands-on, cutting-edge guidance on how directors can power success—and avoid traps. David and Debra Brown are world-class experts; their new book earns a place on director desks everywhere.

Stephen Davis, Ph.D.
Associate Director and Senior Fellow
Harvard Law School Programs on Corporate Governance and Institutional Investors